# NEVERMORE: A Book of Hours

MEDITATIONS ON EXTINCTION

# Other Books by David Day

## Natural History and Ecology
The Doomsday Book of Animals
The Whale War
The Eco Wars
The Encyclopedia of Vanished Species
True Tales
Noah's Choice
Green Penguin Book Guide
The Complete Rhinoceros

## Poetry
The Cowichan
Many Voices:
Canadian Indian Poetry (Editor)
The Scarlet Coat Serial
The Animals Within
Gothic
Visions of St. Louis the Métis
Just Say 'No' to Family Values

## History
History & Literature:
Heritage Anthology (Editor)
Myth and Mountains:
Heritage Anthology (Editor)
Men of the Forest:
Heritage Anthology (Editor)

## Children's Fiction and Poetry
The Emperor's Panda
The Swan Children
The Sleeper
Aska's Animals
The Big Lie
The Walking Catfish
Aska's Birds
The Wolf Children
The King of the Woods
Tippu
Aska's Sea Creatures

## Fantasy and Mythology
The Burroughs Bestiary
A Tolkien Bestiary
Castles
Tolkien: The Illustrated Encyclopedia
Tolkien's Ring
The Tolkien Companion
A to Z of Tolkien
The Quest for King Arthur
The Hobbit Companion
Tolkien's World

# NEVERMORE: A Book of Hours

## MEDITATIONS ON EXTINCTION

BY **David Day**

ILLUSTRATED BY
**Tim Bramfitt**
**Peter Hayman**
**Mick Loates**
**Maurice Wilson**

FOURFRONT EDITIONS

The engraving of the Dutch in Mauritius (1601) is by the celebrated Flemish engraver Johann Theodor de Bry of Liege (1561-1623).

Cover and Book Design: Julie McNeill, McNeill Design Arts
Editor: Allan Briesmaster

*To Allan Thornton and the Agents of the E.I.A., Watchmen of the Wilderness*

**Library and Archives Canada Cataloguing in Publication**

Day, David, 1947-
    Nevermore : a book of hours / written by David Day and illustrated by Maurice Wilson ... [et al.].

Issued also in electronic format.
ISBN 978-1-926802-68-8

    I. Wilson, Maurice, 1914-1987  II. Title.

PS8557.A93N48 2012           C813'.54           C2011-906253-4

Fourfront Editions
Quattro Books
720 Bathurst Street, Suite 200
Toronto, Ontario  M5S 2R4

Printed in Canada

# INTRODUCTION

**NEVERMORE: *A Book of Hours*** has been conceived in the form of a twenty-four hour vigil. Each hour is dedicated to one now-vanished animal species. And each of these hourly meditations is divided into four parts: *Illustration, Reportage, Commentary,* and *Elegy.*

*Illustration:* an original commissioned portrait of each species by one of this book's four distinguished wildlife artists: Tim Bramfitt, Peter Hayman, Mick Loates and Maurice Wilson.

*Reportage:* testimonies by witnesses – who were often the first (or last) to see these animals alive – in the form of monologues taken from naturalists' journals, explorers' ships' logs, travellers' memoirs.

*Commentary:* notations on the testimonies, the witnesses and the animal species which attempt to give them a scientific and historic context.

*Elegy:* original elegies composed in poetic conventions and forms related to each animal's geographic and cultural environment.

In these epicedia, I am at one with Gary Snyder, who in his *Turtle Island,* wrote: "I am a poet who has preferred not to distinguish in poetry between nature and humanity." In this book, human history and natural history are not separate disciplines: humans and animals share a common and interactive history.

Through the reportage and commentaries here, the reader will see how the fates of these animals are directly linked to individuals and events in human history: Julius Caesar with the Aurochs, Xenophon with the Assyrian Onager, Marco Polo with the Elephant Bird, Christopher Columbus with the Eskimo Curlew, Hernando Cortez with the American Bison, Jacques Cartier with the Great Auk, Samuel de Champlain with the Passenger Pigeon, Captain Cook with the Hawaiian O-O, Vitus Bering with Steller's Sea Cow, Charles Darwin with the Antarctic Wolf-Fox.

In the reportage, I have extracted what might almost be seen as "prose poems" from the chronicles of historic witnesses because these authentic voices often convey that sense of the astonishment experienced in those first encounters with these newly discovered creatures; and – as often – a sense of pathos with their ultimate passing.

*NEVERMORE: A Book of Hours* is an adaptation of the *Agrega,* a Coptic – or Ancient Egyptian – word meaning "Book of Hours." The *Agrega* is primarily used today by the Coptic Orthodox Church as a schedule for observing hours of prayer, instruction and meditation – and is comparable to the medieval Roman Catholic *Horae,* a Latin word meaning "Book of Hours."

Books of Hours were the most common type of surviving medieval illuminated manuscripts and personal devotional manuals. They were variable in content but all contained a schedule of hourly readings and prayers adopted from the daily rounds of monastic devotion known as the "canonical hours," as well as being a calendar of prayers for saints and martyrs and a vigil for the souls of the dead.

In *NEVERMORE: A Book of Hours*, the day is divided into eight Coptic canonical hours, and each of these is divided into three watches. Each watch is then assigned an "animal martyr" as the focus of meditation in order to cover the full twenty-four hours of this vigil.

The Coptic *Agrega* was chosen in preference to the Latin *Horae* largely because the – now extinct – Coptic language is actually a demotic form of Egyptian hieroglyphics, and is linked to the Ancient Egyptian *Book of the Dead.* These "coffin texts" used a similar structure of hours for the passage of the souls of the dead through the afterlife.

This book is a requiem to vanished animals which I have tracked down in the museums and institutes around the world. Over the years I have touched the Aurochs horn, the feathers of the Passenger Pigeon, the pelt of the Shamanu, and the amulet of the Dodo's skull. I have seen mounted specimens and preserved skins of the Bali Tiger, the Tarpan and the Thylacine. I have observed trophy heads of the Barbary Lion, the Blue Buck and the Quagga. And I have been amazed by the gigantic thigh bones of the Moa, the massive rib cage of the 7-ton Steller's Sea Cow, and the phenomenal two-gallon Elephant Bird egg.

These are now as much mythical animals as the dragon and the unicorn, but here I have attempted to give them a form of life in the only place they may now exist – the human imagination.

# CONTENTS

## PRIME

# TERCE

FIRST WATCH 9 A.M.

## THE BULL OF HEAVEN | 40

*Aurochs – Bos primigenius – 1627*

✦

Gilgamesh Poet
Julius Caesar
Pliny the Elder
Benedyct Fulinski

✦

**Taurus**


SECOND WATCH 10 A.M.

## THE HORSES OF DAWN | 46

*Tarpan – Equus feras feras – 1887*

✦

Herodotus
Max Toppen
Harold J. E. Peake
Otto Antonius

✦

**The Centaurs**


THIRD WATCH 11 A.M.

## THE LIONS OF ROME | 52

*Atlas Golden Lion – Panthera leo leo – 1922*

✦

Herodotus
Pliny the Elder
Eliakim Littell
Alfred Edward Pease

✦

**The Lion's Gate**

# SEXT

## THE SEA ELEPHANT |58

*Steller's Sea Cow – Hydrodamalis gigas – 1767*
✦
Georg Wilhelm Steller
Petr Yakovlev
✦
**Siren Song**


Second Watch 1 P.M.

## THE TERROR BIRD | 64

*Giant Moa – Dinornis maximus – 1850*
✦
Joel S. Polack
Reverend William Williams
William Colenso
Reverend Richard Taylor
✦
**The Excavation**


Third Watch 2 P.M.

## GALAPAGOS MUTTON | 70

*Floreana Tortoise – Chelonoidis nigra nigra – 1876*
✦
William Dampier
Amasa Delano
Admiral David Porter
Charles Darwin
✦
**La Tortuga Negra**

# None

# VESPERS

FIRST WATCH 6 P.M.

## VIKINGS AND GAREFOWL | 100

*Great Auk – Alca (pinguinus) impennis – 1844*
✦

Jacques Cartier
Anthonie Parkhurst
George Cartwright
Professor A. Newton
✦

**Alpha and Omega**


SECOND WATCH 7 P.M.

## DARWIN'S DOGS | 106

*Warrah Wolf-Fox – Disicyon australis – 1876*
✦

Lord John Byron
Dom Pernetty
Charles Darwin
Lt. Colonel Charles Hamilton-Smith
✦

**Warrah's Last Song**


THIRD WATCH 8 P.M.

## COLUMBUS' CURLEWS | 112

*Eskimo Curlew – Numenius borealis – 1985*
✦

Christopher Columbus
John James Audubon
Dr A. S. Packard
Myron H. Swenk
✦

**Cry of the Curlew**

# COMPLINE

FIRST WATCH 9 P.M.

## THE GOLDEN AGE | 120

*Giant Swamphen – Porphyrio albus – 1830*

✦

Surgeon Arthur Bowes
Captain Thomas Gilbert
Dr. James Foulis
Alan McCulloch

✦

**Ovid's Island**


SECOND WATCH 10 P.M.

## THE FEATHERED GODS | 126

*Hawaiian Oahu O-O – Moho apicalis – 1837*

✦

Captain James Cook
Captain George Vancouver
Coenraad Jacob Temminck
J. C. Greenway

✦

**The Ancestors**


THIRD WATCH 11 P.M.

## THE VAN DYKE | 132

*Ivory-billed Woodpecker – Campephilus principalis – 1972*

✦

Mark Cateby
Alexander Wilson
John James Audubon
President Theodore Roosevelt

✦

**The Lord God Bird**

# MIDNIGHT

FIRST WATCH 12 P.M.

## SCREAM OF THE QUAGGA | 138

*Quagga – Equus quagga quagga – 1883*
✦
George Edwards
William John Burchell
Jared Diamond
✦
**Horses of the Sun**


SECOND WATCH 1 A.M.

## XENOPHON'S ONAGERS | 144

*Assyrian Onager – Equus hemionus hemippus – 1930*
✦
Xenophon
Sir Austen Layard
J. E. T. Aitchison
William Ridgeway
Otto Antonius
✦
**The Walls of Nineveh**


THIRD WATCH 2 A.M.

## OUT OF DREAMTIME | 152

*Toolache Wallaby – Wallabia greyi – 1940*
✦
Sir Joseph Banks
John Gould
Professor F. Wood Jones
✦
**Prayer of the Winabaraku**

# VEIL

*History is not the past. It is the consciousness*
*of the past used for present purposes.*

– E. H. Carr

# THE DODO AND THE PHOENIX

# DODO – 1680 – *Raphus cucullatus*

Sir Thomas Herbert – 1629
## *Some Yeares Travaile,* Mauritius

First, here and here only is generated the Dodo, which for shape and rareness may antagonize the Phoenix of Arabia: her body is round and fat, few weigh less than fifty pound, are reputed of more for wonder then for food. Her visage darts forth melancholy, as sensible of Nature's injurie in framing so great a body to be guided with complementall wings, so small and impotent, that they serve only to prove her a bird. The halfe of her head is naked seeming coucred with a fine vaile, her bill is crooked downwards, in midst is the thrill, from which part to the end tis of a light greene, mixt with pale yellow tincture; her eyes are small and like to Diamonds, round and rowling; her clothing downy feathers, her traine three small plumes, short and inproportionable, her legs suting to her body, her punces sharpe, her appetite strong and greedy.

Sir Thomas Herbert was appointed by King Charles I to the first English ambassadorial mission to the court of the Shah of the Persian Empire. This mission (1627-29) was an attempt to negotiate a silk trade route (bypassing the Ottoman Turkish Empire) through lands and waters controlled by the Persians. It was on his return journey – via India and Africa – that Herbert's ship *The Hart* stopped in Mauritius and he wrote this first account of the Dodo in English.

The Dodo was the world's largest member of the pigeon family: a giant flightless dove the weight of two large domestic turkeys. The Portuguese were the first Europeans to briefly encounter the Dodo in 1507, but the Dutch were the first to record its existence in 1581, and name it *Dodoor* because it resembled a gigantic version of the Dutch Little Grebe or *Dodaers*, meaning "plump-arse." Sometimes called the "Devil's Chicken," the Dodo's desirability as food for sailors varied with the seasons. When fruit was abundant, it was succulent, but during the lean season, the flesh was very tough and ill-tasting.

The claim that "dodo" is derived from the Old Portuguese *duodo* meaning "fool" appears to be without foundation. A more recent theory suggests the name was simply imitative of its 2-note pigeon-like call: "doo-doo." The Dodo's reputation as a creature "unfit" for survival seems odd considering its evolution and survival over five million years; or twice as long as humans have existed.

# WHITE DODO – 1770 – *Victorianis imperialis*

James Tatton – 1631
### *Voyage of Captain Carleton,* Reunion

There is a store of Land-fowl, both small and great, plenty of Doves, great Parrots and such like; and a great fowl of the bigness of a Turkey, very fat, and so short-winged that they cannot fly, being white, and in a manner tame; and so are all other fowles, as having not been troubled or feared with shot.

Dodos were originally believed to have inhabited all three of the Mascarenes: those remote Indian Ocean islands of Mauritius, Rodriguez and Reunion. Fought over by the Portuguese, Dutch, French and British, Rodriguez was eventually successfully colonized by the French East Indian Company. An island with an area of just 110 sq. km., it was inhabited by 60,000 plantation slaves. Like all the Mascarenes, Reunion originally had no land mammals and virtually no predators, but was rapidly invaded by feral cats, dogs, rats, monkeys, pigs and goats, all of whom fed on the indigenous species. The result has been that virtually all of the Mascarenes' endemic animal species and nearly half of its endemic plant species are either endangered or extinct.

Just as the Dodo is on the Mauritius coat of arms, the White Dodo has become the emblematic bird of Reunion. Indeed, in the 1990's the national television network adopted it as the hero of a major animated television series. However, recent archaeological excavations have proved that the legendary White Dodo of Reunion was not a Dodo at all.

It was, in fact, a White Flightless Ibis – *Threskiornis solitarius* – which became extinct in 1770. This large white flightless bird of Reunion was related to the Sacred Ibis of Egypt. A remarkable and unique species, but it was not a member of the Rhaphidae family of the Mauritius Dodo and the Rodriguez Solitaire.

# DODO – 1680 – *Raphus cucullatus*

Sir Hamon L'Estrange – 1638
**L'Estrange Diaries, London, England**

Upon a street there was a house near Lincoln Fields where I discovered the picture of a strange fowle hung out upon a clothe. Upon paying for entry, there I saw on display a great fowl, bigger than the largest Turkey Cock, but stouter and thicker and of a more erect state. The keeper called it a Dodo, and in the end of a chimney in the chambers there lay a heape of large pebble stones, whereof hee gave it many in our sight, some as big as nutmegs and the keeper told us she eats them conducing to digestion.

Sir Hamon L'Estrange was an English theologian who while walking in central urban London stopped at a house to examine a live captive Dodo. L'Estrange's interest in the Dodo may also have been provoked by Herbert's account. His *Some Yeares Travaile* was a popular book of the day.

Curiously, upon its demise, this Dodo was acquired as a stuffed exhibit by John Tradescant (creator of Charles II's "physics garden") for his "cabinet of curiosities." This was eventually integrated with the collection of the antiquarian Jacob Ashmole to form the basis of the Ashmolean Museum in Oxford. Here, the world's only intact Dodo was kept, until the deteriorating specimen was accidentally incinerated, although fortunately the head and one foot were rescued. The excavations of the dry swamp bed of the Mare Aux Songes in Mauritius resulted in the discovery of numerous new skeletal remains of Dodos in 1865; and in 2005.

Still one might argue that there is a phoenix-like aspect to this story, as this famous specimen in Oxford was the inspiration for the creation of Lewis Carroll's fictional Dodo in his *Alice in Wonderland* (1865). The Dodo was a private joke the author shared with Alice about himself. Carroll (a.k.a. Charles Dodgson) suffered from stuttering, and often introduced himself as Mr. Do-Do-Dodgson.

The Dodo was the subject of a number of paintings by European artists: most notably Roeland Savery's iconic bird of 1626. However, the Mughul artist, Mansur of Naggash – in the court of the Emperor Jehangir in Goa – created the most well-observed painting of a Dodo drawn from life, sometime between 1610 to 1624.

## SOLITAIRE DODO – 1780 – *Pezohaps solitarius*

Francois Leguat of Bresse – 1708
### *A New Voyage to the East Indies,* Rodriguez

The Females are wonderfully beautiful, some fair, some brown; I call them fair, because they are the colour of fair Hair. They have a sort of Peak, like a Widow's upon their Beak, which is of a dun colour. No one feather is straggling from the other. The Feathers on their Thighs are round like shells at one end, and being there very thick, have an agreeable effect. They have two Risings on the Craws, and Feathers are whiter there than the rest, which lively represents the fine bosom of a Beautiful Woman. They walk with so much stateliness and good Grace, that one cannot help admiring and loving them.

During the reign of Louis XIV, Francois Leguat was forced to flee to Holland; where in 1691, along with other prominent Huguenots, he was persuaded to attempt to establish a new French Protestant Refuge Colony in the "New Eden" of Reunion. They were promised two ships to service the colony of L'ile Eden, but instead they found themselves on a single small frigate that deserted them on Rodriguez Island.

After two years in the failed Rodriguez colony, Leguat and the others escaped on a small boat to Mauritius, and were imprisoned by the Dutch both in Mauritius and Batavia for several years. At the age of 70 the wandering Leguat found sanctuary in London, and published his *Voyages – 1689-98* in French, English and Dutch editions. Leguat's account of his harrowing desert island adventures included descriptions of the Dodo that were entirely at odds with any previous tales; however, they have proved to be extremely accurate. Leguat recorded their mating rituals. Noting that these birds mated for life, he also remarked how they were far from passive when it came to protecting their young.

The Solitaire was the intelligent, beautiful Cinderella of the Dodo (Raphidae) family. Nonetheless, these characteristics did not save it from sharing the fate of its less charming cousin. Nor did it save at least two dozen other indigenous Mascarene species (pigeons, parrots, rails, tortoises, snakes, and skinks) from extinction.

# LA MARE AUX SONGES

## Dodo – 1680

The first ships appear off these shores
Just as Galileo's telescope reveals
The dry seas of the moon

Now, we dig and search for relics: a beak or a bone
Of a creature that will be nevermore forever

Something in the Dodo's foolish Mona Lisa smile
Provoked Mogul artists and Dutch masters

And provokes us still, as we discover
A human skull with an equally enigmatic grin
Next to the bones of this flightless giant dove

It is impossible to stave off thoughts
Of our own eventual eclipse

How will we be seen: tragic or comic?
Hubristic, or an evolutionary mistake?

In what arid sea and by whom will our relics be found
When our monuments crumble away?

I try to imagine Alexander or Ozymandias
But instead, as darkness falls
On the edge of this dry "Sea of Dreams"

The moon with the bone-white face of Pagliacci
Looms up before me

Only then do I recall his murdered wife
*Columbina*, meaning "Dove"

And hear: *"Le commedia e finita!"*
God's judgement, delivered in Caruso's terrible
Perfect voice

# SINBAD AND THE RUKH

# ELEPHANT BIRD or RUKH – 1700
## *Aepyornis maximus*

Marco Polo – 1298
## *Travels: Concerning the Isle of Madastar,* Madagascar

The people of this island report that at a certain season of the year, an extraordinary giant bird, which they call a Rukh, makes an appearance in the southern regions. The Grand Khan having heard this extraordinary relation, sent messengers to the island to enquire about these curious matters.

Marco Polo's account of Madagascar was written in 1294 after his return by ship via the Indies and the coast of Africa from the court of the Great Khan. Arab traders had for centuries before Europeans traded along the coast of Africa and long believed Madagascar to be the home of this legendary giant Rukh or Roc. Anyone familiar with the stories of Sinbad and Aladdin from the *Thousand and One Nights* was acquainted with this extraordinary bird; but its celebrity is not confined to that work.

*"Rukh,"* says one Arabic and Persian Dictionary, "is the name of a monstrous bird, which is said to have powers sufficient to carry off a live rhinoceros." Its existence seems to have been universally credited in the East; and those Arabian navigators with whom Marco Polo conversed did not hesitate to attest to its existence.

However, it was not until 1866 that a complete skeleton of this bird was discovered. And it was not until then that the bird's size was calculated. It may have not been the size of the mythical Roc, but with a height of ten feet and weight of half a ton, it was certainly the largest and heaviest bird to ever walk the earth.

The name Elephant Bird seems somewhat peculiar, as Madagascar has never had an indigenous elephant population. It does serve to indicate the bird's huge size, or perhaps is a reference to Sinbad's legend, wherein it was so large it was capable of carrying off elephants. Its scientific name, *Aepyornis,* means "tall or lofty bird."

Sieur Etienne de Flacourt – 1658
*History of the Great Island of Madagascar*

The Vouron Patra is a giant bird that lives in the country of the Amphrates people in the south of Madagascar. The great eggs of these birds are used to store water. So that people of these places may not catch it, the Vouron Patra seeks the loneliest places.

France took possession of Madagascar in 1642, and Flacourt was the island's first governor and a keen naturalist. Shortly after completing his *History*, Flacourt was killed by Algerian pirates while on a return voyage to France, and there were no other written accounts of this bird for nearly two centuries.

Then, in 1832, Victor Sganzin, a French artillery officer stationed in Madagascar, found one native family using as a water bowl half an eggshell a foot in diameter. Upon querying, he was told that such eggs were quite common in certain parts of the island. Sganzin purchased the egg and sent it to Jules Verreaux, a French collector of curiosities in Cape Town. Verreaux excitedly sailed for Paris with his discovery. Sadly, a terrible storm struck and Verreaux, the ship and the Roc's egg all sank beneath the waves.

The Elephant Bird's egg is the largest that any egg could possibly grow. It is estimated that any egg larger would have to have a shell so thick that it could not be broken by a hatching chick. Over the last century a considerable number of these eggs have been discovered, the largest measuring a metre in circumference with a fluid capacity of two imperial gallons – equal to 200 chicken eggs, or three times the size of the largest dinosaur eggs.

Ship Surgeon John Joliffe – 1848
*Voyage to the Spice Islands,* **Indian Ocean**

Monsieur Dumarele, a merchant of Reunion, spoke of having seen at Port Leven the shell of an enormous egg, the production of an unknown bird inhabiting the wilds of the country, which held the almost incredible quantity of *thirteen wine quart bottles of fluid!!!* He having himself carefully measured the quantity. Dumarele offered to purchase the egg from the natives, but they declined selling it, stating that it belonged to their chief, and that they could not dispose of it without his permission. The natives said that the egg was found in the jungle, and observed that such eggs were very rarely met with, and that the bird which produces them is still more rarely seen.

John Joliffe was the surgeon on a British ship that stopped in Madagascar in 1848, where he was befriended by Dumarele, a trader from Reunion, who traded extensively along the Madagascar coast. Joliffe was somewhat sceptical, but reported his account to the British ornithologist, Hugh Strickland. Lacking physical evidence, Strickland replied: "The sight of one sound egg would be worth a thousand theories."

Two years later, in 1850, an awe-struck Geoffroy Saint-Hilaire, the director of the Paris Zoo, received not one, but three "sound eggs" along with a crate of massive bones of this bird. These were collected by Captain Abadie, master of a French merchant ship recently returned from Madagascar. The largest measured approximately 13" by 16" in diameter and had a fluid capacity of nine litres.

Arab and Malay settlers came to settle Madagascar about a millennium before the French, and began to cut down its virgin forest and invade the nesting grounds that once were the sandy shores of Madagascar. When the final blow fell – whether by gun, spear or fire – is not known, although by 1700 the Elephant Bird was almost certainly extinct.

The discovery of Elephant Bird eggs in the late 19th century prompted H.G. Wells to write a little-known pre-*Jurassic Park* short story entitled "Aepyornis Island."

# THE RUKH'S EGG

### Elephant Bird or Rukh – 1700

1.

O Kings of the Ages – what deeds have been done?
What taboos broken and whirlwinds unleashed?

For Alá al-Din's wish to possess the Rukh's Egg
The mighty Slave of the Lamp turned
On his Master with the threat of annihilation:

> *"O Ignorant Man, Know ye not what ye ask?*
> *Know ye not from its outward form*
> *What is held within the Rukh's Egg?*
> *For this wish I should slaughter you!"*

And then came the Destroyer of Worlds,
The Plunderer of Palaces, the Despoiler of Cities.


2.

And yet, for all else the great Jin
Answered Alá al-Din, with a flourish:
> *"To hear is to obey!"*

In a single night, the Slave of the Lamp
Raised a grand pavilion all built of alabaster,
Of Sumaki-marble, of jasper and jet and jade.

And beneath the great dome was a belvedere
With the latticed casements of four and twenty windows
Glazed and glittering with rubies and with emeralds.

And therein, Alá al-Din was placed upon a golden throne
And guarded by mamuluks and eunuchs
And served by handmaids and dancers
And eight and forty slave girls.

And all were covered in raiments of silk
And gold brocades and or frayed cloths
Embroidered with pearls and precious gems

Lit with candles of camphor and ambergris
And filled with the sounding of trumpets
And beating of kettle drums.

But all this ended with Alá al-Din's fatal wish.

For at that utterance, from the abyss a voice thundered:

> "By Allah, ye deserve that I reduce you to ashes
> This very moment and scatter you upon the wind.
>
> "Better ye wish to hang the mother of the Prophet
> From the pavilion dome."

3.

Once prized above all things,
What was the meaning of the Rukh's Egg?
What made it the one great taboo?

Like Alá al-Din, we are still unknowing
Of its inner from its outer significance.

What was the secret of this talisman
Known only to the Wise?

What is here to be discovered?
What fatal prophecy is to be revealed?

The Rukh's Egg is like a planet unto itself,
But bone white, barren as the moon

And now hollow, bereft of all life:
Vision of our world to come.

# LA GRANDE CARAPACE

# MAURITIAN GIANT TORTOISES – 1700
## *Cylindraspis inepta; Cylindraspis trisserata*

Sir Thomas Herbert – 1630
### *Some Yeares Travaile,* **Mauritius**

The Ile has no humane inhabitants. Those creatures that possesse it, have it on condition to pay tribute to such ships as famine, or foule weather force to anchor there. Here are land Tortoyses so great that they will creepe with two men's burthen, and serve more for sport than service or solemne Banquet.

Sir Thomas Herbert, who gave us the first descriptions of the Dodo in English, also wrote this early account of the similarly doomed Mauritius Giant Tortoises. There were two species of giant tortoise on Mauritius, but sadly Herbert was quite wrong about them being unpalatable. The French and Portuguese slaughtered tens of thousands for meat for their crews on their Indian Ocean ships. On Mauritius, one Abbé Pengré noted that, while on the island, his diet consisted entirely of *"soupe de tortue, tortue enficasee, tortes en doube, tortue en godiveau, oeufs de tortue, foie de tortue, tells etaient Presque nos unique ragouts."* Predictably, both species soon became extinct.

Curiously, after his return to England, Sir Thomas Herbert became embroiled in the civil war (on the side of Cromwell), and found himself watching over another endangered species: the British monarchy. Herbert was appointed servant and jailer to the imprisoned Charles I. During the King's last months, Herbert was the monarch's sole attendant, and accompanied the King to the scaffold. Later, after the phoenix-like resurrection of the monarchy, Herbert was made a baronet by Charles II for his kindness toward Charles I, and wrote his compassionate *Threnodia Carolina – Last Days of Charles I.* The *Threnodia* was published in 1678, a date that almost exactly coincides with the extinction of Herbert's Dodo, and is within two decades of the same fate befalling the Mauritius Tortoises.

# REUNION GIANT TORTOISES – 1773
## *Cylindraspis indica; Cylindraspis borboica*

Marquis Henri Du Quesne – 1689
### *Memoire – Projet de Republique a L'ile Eden,* Reunion

There are vast numbers of Tortoises: their flesh is very delicate and the fat better than butter or the best oil, for all kinds of sauces which is also a good remedy for many ills. The biggest ones can carry a man with greater ease than a man can carry them. Each animal usually makes two pots of oil and twenty people can be fed from one of these turtles.

Here the Marquis Henri Du Quesne writes glowingly of one of the many bounteous natural treasures awaiting colonists he is commissioned to transport to the L'ile Eden – or Reunion – the largest of the three Mascarene islands. As on Mauritius, the two species of Giant Tortoise on Reunion were slaughtered in the thousands to supply meat for traders.

However, this new Eden for the exiled and endangered Huguenots failed. In fact, Du Quesne was the naval commander of the frigate *La Hirondelle,* whom Francois Leguat accuses of abandoning the colonists (including himself) on the uninhabited Rodriguez.

To give some idea of the number of giant tortoises once inhabiting these islands, it should be observed that in the widely scattered array of islands in the Seychelles Group, there is the tiny islet of Aldabra Atoll. Measuring less than eighteen by seven miles (most of which is a lagoon), it was inhabited by over one hundred thousand tortoises. Uninhabited by humans and without a safe harbour or sufficient fresh water, Aldabra was the habitat of the only surviving species of Indian Ocean Tortoise (*Aldabrachelys gigantean*).

## RODRIGUEZ GIANT TORTOISES – 1800
### *Cylindraspis vosmaeri; Cylindraspis peltastes*

Francois Leguat of Bresse – 1708
### *A New Voyage to the East Indies,* Rodriguez

There are such plenty of Land Turtles on this Isle, that sometimes you see 2-3000 of them in a Flock; so that you can go above a hundred paces on their backs without setting foot on the ground. They meet together in the evening in shady places, and lie so close, that one would think those spots were paved with them. …We all unanimously agreed 'twas better than the best Butter in Europe. To anoint one's self with this Oil is an excellent Remedy for Surfeits, Colds, Cramps, and several other Distempers. The Liver of the animal is extraordinarily delicate, 'tis so Delicious that one may say of it, it always carries its own Sauce with it, dress it how you will.

During the reign of Louis XIV, Francois Leguat was forced to flee to Holland, where, in 1691, along with other Huguenots, he was persuaded to establish a new Protestant Colony in the "New Eden" of Reunion. They were promised two ships, but instead were deserted on Rodriguez.

In 1693, after two years as the only inhabitants on an island 40 miles square, they built a boat and sailed to Mauritius, where they were imprisoned before they escaped to Batavia, where they were once again imprisoned. When finally released by the Dutch after seven years, Leguat and two others were the only survivors of L'ile Eden.

Mahé de Labourdonnais – 1730

*French East India Company Decree,* **Rodriguez**

All ship's captains must be forbidden to send out their boats to collect tortoises without informing the island commandants and stating the numbers they require.

Though pirates and occasional Dutch naval ships had been taking tortoises from Rodriguez for some time, it was not until Leguat's memoirs were published in 1708 that the island came to be regarded as a meat reservoir for the French and English navies. By 1730, Reunion Tortoises were becoming scarce and the Mauritian herds had entirely vanished. This decree was made – not so much to preserve the island tortoises – as to attempt to enforce a monopoly on their harvesting. In any case, the decree was ignored and the tortoise populations continued to rapidly plummet.

Rodriguez was later re-colonized by the Mauritius governor Mahé de Labourdonnais with a small group of soldiers, lascars and slaves who were required to gather live tortoises. They sent 10,000 tortoises off annually. Some shiploads were of 6,000 tortoises and on several occasions three quarters of the cargo perished. The last big haul was in January 1768 when L'Heureux took off 1215 "carosses" (the largest size tortoises).

In 1791, the last overseer, Jean de Valgny, died on Rodriguez, a virtual castaway dependent for food for himself and two slaves largely on the generosity of visiting ships. For the tortoises were gone and, with them, went France's interest in Rodriguez. The last tortoises ever seen were two down at the bottom of an inaccessible ravine in 1795.

# MARION'S GIANT TORTOISE – 1929
## *Cylindraspis sumeri*

Albert Gunther – 1875
**Letter to *The Times*, London**

As to the origin of the large tortoise – known as *Marion's Tortoise* – living in Mauritius… I am afraid positive evidence will be obtained only when, after the death of the animal, the bones can be compared with those of the other Mascarene tortoises. But I trust that great care will be taken in prolonging the existence of one of the oldest terrestrial creatures and, probably, the last of its race.

Marion's Tortoise was named after Marc-Joseph Marion du Fresne who was a renowned naval officer, trader and explorer. In 1766, the Chevalier Marion brought this captive tortoise from Reunion to Mauritius. There in Port Louis the captain served as harbour master, and upon his departure, placed the tortoise in the care of the French Garrison. Marion's Tortoise remained there until 1810, when the British bombarded Port Louis and forced a French surrender. During the attack, Marion's Tortoise was wounded – scarring its shell – but fortunately recovered to serve as the British Royal Artillery mascot for another half century before It came to the attention of Albert Gunther of the zoology department of the British Museum through correspondence with Captain Samuel Pasfield Oliver who served as an artillery officer on Mauritius.

In the months following his letter to *The Times*, Albert Gunther received photographs and numerous reliable accounts that proved beyond doubt that Marion's Tortoise was indeed the last living Mascarene Tortoise – and probably the only one still living after 1800. It was largely due to Gunther's persistence in gathering the public support of Walter Baron Rothschild, Sir Joseph Hooker, Richard Owen and Charles Darwin that any Giant Land Tortoises elsewhere in the world survived into the twentieth century.

Marion's Tortoise lived on as the Royal Artillery mascot until 1929, when he died as the result of a fall down a well. He had been in captivity for 163 years. His actual age is unknown, but as he was brought to Mauritius as a large mature adult, he must have survived for at least two entire centuries.

# METHUSELAH'S TURTLE

### Marion's Giant Tortoise – 1929

In the year 1929, Marion's Tortoise
Suffered a fatal fall

He was two hundred years old
If he was a day, when he toppled
From the Mauritian garrison's parapet

Who among us could imagine
What it was like?

> *Death is before me today*
> *Like the sweet scent of myrrh*
> *Rising from a thorn tree in the desert*

In 1766, a decade before the American Revolution –
Already full-grown and the last of his race –
He was brought from the Isle of Rodriguez
To the garrison by the Chevalier de Marion

He outlived the last of the Bourbon Kings,
The Emperor Napoleon on his lonely isle,
Bismarck, and Queen Victoria

He kept an even keel
Even as the Titanic turned turtle

And survived the years of the Great War
That ended the power of the Kaiser,
The Ottomans and the Russian Czars

> *Death is before me today*
> *Like a strong wind filling*
> *The sails of a great ship*

To the French and English in the garrison
He was the soldier's mascot: the embodiment
Of steadfastness and endurance

And the island's Hindu lascars and slaves
Had an ancient legend ready-made for him:

He was Chukwa, the Great Tortoise
Upon whose back was heaped
The weight of the whole world

And perhaps from their own enslavement
Through generations of exile and captivity,
They understood something of his suffering

> *Death is before me today*
> *Like the desire of an ancient prisoner*
> *To see his home again*

The Tortoise's fall
Was an unlikely accident

Blind or not, after a century and a half
The garrison's corridors were no mystery

His own time had long passed

The weight of the world
Did indeed rest upon his back

The air above his carapace was empty
Yet heavier for all that with the weight of time

Not quite the immortal Chukwa
He was not the Spiritus Mundi

Not the footstool of Venus
Not Methuselah's Pet

But only a lonely mortal tortoise

It was time to join the others
This was the end of his race

It was time to see his home again

# THE BULL OF HEAVEN

# AUROCHS OR WILD OX – 1627 – *Bos primigenius*

Gilgamesh Poet – 2100 BC
***Epic of Gilgamesh,* Sumeria**

Ishtar led the Bull of Heaven
Down into the world.

When the Bull of Heaven bellowed
The earth shook and quaked:
Lakes and streams were emptied
And the Euphrates stopped its flow.

When the Bull of Heaven bellowed again
And its great hoof struck the ground:
The earth cracked open
And into that deadly abyss fell
The armies of the King of Uruk.

The Aurochs or Wild Ox first appears in literature in that first epic of the human race, *Gilgamesh* (Mesopotamia – 2100 BC), as the "Bull of Heaven" belonging to Anu the King of the Gods is lent to his daughter Ishtar, who wishes to use it to destroy the hero Gilgamesh, the King of Uruk. The Aurochs is also referred to as the *Reem* in the Bible, and as the British traveller Canon Tristram wrote in 1884, "on the Assyrian monuments its chase is represented as the greatest feat of hunting in the time of the dynasties of Nineveh."

In Greek mythology, the Aurochs was the avatar of the thunderbolt god, Zeus, and the god of earthquakes, Poseidon. In the 5th century BC, the Greek historian Herodotus, in his *The Persian Wars,* wrote: "That whole region [of Thrace] is full of lions and wild bulls with gigantic horns which are brought into Greece." In the earlier Minoan civilization of Crete many images of these massive wild bulls being used in the spectacular sport of bull jumping were painted on the walls of the palace of Knossos.

Julius Caesar – 65 BC
*De Bello Gallico,* Gaul

They are but little less than Elephants in size, and are of the species, colour and form of a bull. Their strength is very great, and also their speed. They spare neither man nor beast that they see. They cannot be brought to endure the sight of men, nor can they be tamed, even when taken young. The people who take them in pitfalls assiduously destroy them: and young men harden themselves in this labour, and exercise themselves in this kind of chase; and those who have killed a great number – the horns being publicly exhibited in evidence of the fact – obtain great honour. The horns in amplitude, shape and species, differ much from the horns of our oxen. They are much sought after; and after having been edged with silver at their mouths they are used for drinking vessels at great feasts.

The Aurochs or Wild Ox was known to Caesar as the *Ur* or *Uras.* Measuring six and a half feet at the shoulder, the Aurochs was the archetypal wild bull, as its Latin name *Bos primigenius* suggests. It was from the Aurochs that all our domestic cattle are derived. It is the source of what was the single most important animal domestication in the evolution of agriculture-based civilizations.

Recent DNA research indicates there were at least three subspecies of Aurochs. Two were the Indian Aurochs from which the "humped" cattle of India are descended, and the North African Aurochs from which the "humpless" cattle of the Near East are descended. What survived in a wild state into historic times in Europe was this terrifying, primeval, and untameable Giant Wild Ox.

Pliny the Elder – 65 AD
***Natural History,* Rome**

Scythia produces but very few animals in consequence of the scarcity of shrubs. Germany, which lies close adjoining it, has not many animals, though it has some very fine kinds of wild oxen: the Bison, which has a mane, and the Urus.

The hunting of the Aurochs seems to have been regarded as the exclusive right of kings and aristocrats among the Germanic peoples. In the 9th century, Charlemagne hunted Aurochs in the forests near Aix-la-Chapelle; while in the German epic the *Niebelungenlied,* we learn that the hero Siegfried slaughtered four of these mighty beasts near Worms in the 12th century.

The Aurochs was sometimes confused with that other giant of the European forests: the Wisent or European Bison. Both of these beasts are famously and frequently portrayed in hunting scenes in prehistoric cave paintings. It is instructive to realize that although populations of both these massive quadrupeds were hunted by man for at least 40,000 years, it took the advent of firearms to result in their extinction.

Benedyct Fulinski – 1627
*Fulinski Manuscript XVII,* **Poland**

A century ago, King Sigismund III Vasa, seeing the imminent danger of a quick and total extermination of the Aurochs, proclaimed orders with the object of protecting the feeding grounds of these animals, the number of which at this time did not amount to more than some ten pieces. Unluckily the enactment of those orders came too late and in consequence the Aurochs disappeared from the lands over the next century.

By 1400, two royal preserves in Poland were the last refuges of the Aurochs. By 1564, there were only 30 surviving animals in the Jaktorowska forest preserve. By 1620, this last herd had dwindled to one last animal. With her death in 1627, after nearly four millennia, the "Bull of Heaven" finally enters the annals of literature – along with the dragon and the griffin – as an entirely (non-existent) mythical creature.

Like the Aurochs, the Wisent was becoming rare by the end of the Middle Ages. By the 1800s, Wisent populations surviving in the wild had dwindled to small herds in only two regions and in two forms. Both the Caucasian Wisent (*Bison bonasus caucasicus*) and the Lithuanian Wisent (*Bison bonasus bonasus*) populations survived because they lived in substantial park reserves under the protection of the Czar of Russia. However, after the Great War and the Russian Revolution, these last animals were no longer protected in imperial reserves, and by 1923, both the Caucasian and Lithuanian Wisent became extinct in the wild. Then, in 1925, an aging bull called Kaukasus, the last of the Caucasian race, died in the Hamburg Zoo.

However, a remarkable captive breeding program by the European Bison Society in the 1920's gathered just 6 captive animals from various zoos, and miraculously saved the Lithuanian race from extinction. Since the end of the Second World War, new parklands were established, and today there are several thousand European Bison of the Lithuanian subspecies roaming woodland reserves in Europe.

# TAURUS

### Aurochs or Wild Ox – 1627

The last black bull's wounding
Was like the bursting
Of an old sun in the belly
His roar betrayed the centuries
Of refusing to tread warily in this world
Flutes were made from his bones
They play them even now
And hunting horns from his ivory crown

In his veins the singing of a hundred
Rapacious birds
He was strength without malice
His forehead was a crushing millstone

Fearful, lordly beast of all the mythologies
Father of the minotaur
A small part of his stubborn blood
Is yet in the fighting bulls of the ring
Who break the bodies of horses and men

His legend is as ancient as the pale moon
But his life now is only a fish's song
And his spirit is steel and flint striking
On a dark and empty plain

# THE HORSES OF DAWN

## TARPAN – 1887 – *Equus feras feras*

Herodotus – 445 BC
### *History of the Persian Wars,* Greece

The third great river in Scythia is Hypanis. This stream rises within the limits of Scythia, and has its source in another vast lake, around which wild white horses graze. The lake is called properly enough, the Mother of the Hypanis.

The Tarpan is the Eurasian Wild Horse or "True Wild Horse" (*Equus feras* or *Equus feras feras*) from which the many breeds of the Domestic Horse (*Equus caballus*) are descended. The name "Tarpan," meaning "Wild Horse," is from a Turkic language (Kyrgyz or Kazakh). It was also known as the *Dzerlik-adu* by the Mongols (and the *Yeh-Ma* by the Chinese). The Tatars and Cossacks, like these others, distinguished the Tarpan wild horse from the feral horse, which they called the *Takja* or *Muzin*. The oldest human records we have of the existence of Tarpans are to be found in cave paintings 20-40,000 years old. The wild horses on the walls of the caves of Lascaux are perfectly-detailed portraits of the Tarpan with its distinctive "Mohawk" mane.

Herodotus in Book Four of *The Persian Wars* concerns himself with Scythia, which he defines as all the lands between the Danube and the Don Rivers. Herodotus credits the nomadic tribesmen there with being the finest horsemen in the world, and Scythia as the one part of the world where true wild horses still roamed in abundance. The region where wild white horses were to be found grazing (and survived until the early 19th century) was probably the region known as the Pripyat Marshes on today's Polish-Belarus-Ukraine border.

Max Toppen – 1870
*History of Mascovia,* Danzig

In the time of the Teutonic Knights, wild horses and other game were hunted for the sake of their skins. In 1543 Duke Albert sent an order to command at Lyck, bidding him take measures for the preservation of wild horses. Proofs of the horse being an object of the chase in Poland and Lithuania are found far into the seventeenth century.

In the forests of Białowieża, Poland, records of the hunting of the Tarpan go back to 1409, when King Władyslaw Jagiello arranged a royal chase in honour of his cousin, Witold of Lithuania. In these immense forests the Tarpan, along with European Bison (Wisent), survived in substantial numbers through most of the 18th century. However, by 1800, the Tarpan had vanished everywhere except on the steppes of Tauria and Cherson. The last herds died out in the Ukraine around 1850, and the last known pure-bred Tarpan was killed near Askamia Nova in Russia on Christmas Day in 1879. Eight years later, the last captive Tarpan died in Poland.

Harold J. E. Peake – 1933
*On the Domestication of the Horse,* **London**

The first mention of the horse is documented before 2000 BC in Babylon, where it is called the 'Ass from the East', but it does not seem to have been introduced into Mesopotamia before the arrival of the Kassite conquerors in 1746 BC. The horse was also well known to the Hittites, who arrived in Asia Minor about 1900 BC from the Northwest. All this evidence tends to show that the horse was used as a means of transport both in Persia and upon the Russian steppe well before 2000 BC. It seems likely that it was first tamed in that part of the world, or still farther east in Mongolia, as early as 3000 BC.

Samuel Gotlieb Gmelin, a German physician, botanist, and explorer of Russia in the days of Catherine the Great, was the first to collect specimens of the Tarpan and make it known to science. In 1766, Gmelin was appointed professor of botany at St. Petersburg, and the next year he was sent on an expedition to study the natural history of the Russian Empire. In his four-volume *Reise Durch Russland,* Gmelin recorded seeing the animals in 1769 in the Brobrovsk region near Voronezh. Gmelin's hunters killed a stallion and two mares and a foal. He described the stallion as "hardly as large as the smallest Russian pony." Gmelin explored the Don and Volga Rivers and the shores of the Caspian Sea. In the Caucasus he was taken hostage by Usmey Khan of Khaitakes, and died in captivity at the age of 29.

In 1784 Pieter Boddaert named the species *Equus ferus,* based on Gmelin's description. This was to distinguish it from its descendants, the 300 or so breeds of the Domestic Horse (*Equus caballus,* as named by Linnaeus in 1758).

Otto Antonius – 1938
*On the Recent Equidae,* Vienna

In times not long before the beginning of historical days there were true wild horses or Tarpan spread over the whole Eurasiatic continent from the Atlantic to the Pacific. The Tarpan was a mouse-dun horse, which the medieval philosopher Albertus Magnus means when he calls the colour of the wild horse 'cinereus', as in ash-coloured. The first Duke of Prussia, Albert von Hohenzollern, sent wild horses as highly esteemed gifts to the Emperor, and also to the Archduke Ferdinand, so there can be no doubt that these horses were truly royal game – like the Urus and the Bison. The last refuge of the Tarpanis in Poland was the great game park of Count Zamoyski. Here they were strictly protected until the civil conflict and severe winter of 1812 made feeding and survival impossible. Franz von Falz-Fein, the owner of the matchless Ascania Nova Zoo, has told the life-history of that last wild horse of Europe, an old one-eyed mare, lingering for years around the feral horses, covered by domestic he-horses, captured, escaped with its filly, and some years later hunted and killed on the ice by the peasants of Agaiman.

Otto Antonius was an Austrian zoologist and palaeontologist who became director of the Tiergarten Schönbrunn in Vienna. An active member of the Zoological Society of London, Antonius was co-founder of modern zoological biology. He was a pioneer in creating modern humane zoo environments and redefining zoos as places to protect and breed endangered species. A key figure in saving the Wisent from extinction, he was also one of the first to attempt "re-breeding" domestic animals back to their wild ancestral stock. At the close of World War II, the Schönbrunn Zoo was nearly destroyed in bombing raids, and with the approach of the Russian Army on 9 April 1945, Antonius and his wife committed suicide.

Antonius' methods were adapted by others and resulted in the successful captive-breeding of the Przewalski Wild Horse (*Equus przewalski* or *Equus feras przewalski*) – the only surviving form of Wild Horse – despite its total extinction in the wild. His concept of "re-breeding" has also resulted in the controversial "reconstruction" of "Tarpan-like" animals that can now be seen in a number of zoos and wildlife refuges.

# THE CENTAURS

## Tarpan – 1887

Little wild horses of the steppes
Straggling tribal men
What has the Emperor
Behind the Great Wall to fear?
He feeds on peacock tongues
His people cover the lands of the world
His power changes the course of rivers
And shapes the face of the earth

He is disturbed by a terrible vision
He fears the image of a demon
With eight limbs
That is fierce and swift

The Tartar horn blows
And the vision
In a whirlwind comes

At the Dragon Gate
At the Ivory Gate
The bowmen mount the towers
But the demons pass by, not against the wall
But around, their brave hearts pounding distance away

It is the frenzy of the little horses
And the savage tribal men
Two creatures made one

The Tartar horn blows
And the Tarpan carries the tribesmen on
The wall is left to the west wind
The yellow axes of the Imperial Guard are untried
The horsemen pass by, pass around
The cities are pyres
The jade images are shattered
The silk of the Imperial banners
Lies tattered beneath the conqueror's hooves

# THE LIONS OF ROME

## ATLAS GOLDEN LION – 1922 – *Panthera leo leo*

Herodotus – 410 BC
### *The Persian Wars,* Greece

That whole region [of Thrace] is full of lions… upon Xerxes' march the camels that carried the provisions of the Persian army were set upon by lions, which left their lairs and came down by night, but spared the men and the beasts of burden, while they made the camels their prey. I marvel what may have been the cause which compelled the lions to leave the other animals untouched and attack the camels, when they had never seen that beast before, or had any experience of it.

The Barbary or Atlas Golden-Mane Lion, as its Latin name *Panthera leo leo* suggests, was the remnant population of the archetypal lion species that once roamed throughout the entire Mediterranean basin. As this curious observation by the Greek historian Herodotus in his *The Persian Wars* (410 BC) confirms, lions were still numerous in Europe in Classical Greek times, and they were certainly still extant in Macedonia in the days of Alexander the Great. The Mediterranean Lion was probably extinct in its northern range of Europe by the time of Julius Caesar's Rome, but remained relatively numerous for most of the next two millennia throughout North Africa – from Egypt to Morocco – until the advent of modern firearms.

Also known as Nubian Lions, these are the same ferocious animals portrayed in Eugène Ferdinand-Victor Delacroix's famous *Lion Hunting in Morocco* (1854), painted two decades after his visit to North Africa. Richard Lydecker, in his *The Game of Africa* (1908), describes the Atlas or Barbary Lion as "very large, dusky ochery, with the mane very thick, long, and extending to the middle of the back, and a thick and heavy mane on the under parts. The males may weigh 500 lbs and measure 10 feet from nose to tip of tail."

Pliny the Elder – 65 AD
*Natural History,* **Rome**

Quintus Scaevola, the son of P. Scaevola, when he was *curule aedile,* was the first to exhibit at Rome a combat of a number of lions; and L. Sylla, who was afterwards Dictator, during his praetorship, gave the spectacle of a fight of one hundred lions with manes. After him, Pompeius Magnus exhibited six hundred lions in the Circus, three hundred and fifteen of which had manes; Caesar, the Dictator, exhibited four hundred.

As H.A. Bryden wrote in his *Great and Small Game of Africa* (1899): "There is little doubt that the Romans drew their chief supply of Lions for the arena and gladiatorial combats from Mauretania and Numidia. Pliny speaks of hundreds at a time being shown by Pompey and Caesar in the Roman arena. This bespeaks a great abundance of Lions in North Africa. Lions still linger here and there in the southeast and southwest of Algeria."

John Bostock, the 1855 translator of Gaius Plinius Secundus' *Natural History*, noted: "Seneca gives an account of this exhibition; he says that the lions were turned loose into the Circus, and that spearmen were sent by King Bocchus, who killed them with darts." Scaevola's title of *curule aedile* was that of a chief magistrate (consul or praetor) of Rome's public works, buildings and games.

Also in North Africa, the Atlas Brown Bear (*Ursus arctos crowtheri*) suffered an almost identical history and fate to that of the Atlas Golden Lion. Herodotus and the Roman writers Virgil, Juvenal and Martial refer to this animal as the "Libyan Bear," while Pliny tells us that in 61 BC Domitius Ahenobarbus brought "one hundred Numidian Bears" to Rome's arenas. As late as 1830, there were live captive Atlas Brown Bears in Morocco and Marseille. In 1841, it was investigated by the Zoological Society and pronounced a rare and unique species or subspecies "very different from any other bear." It became extinct about 1870.

Eliakim Littell – 1882
*English Mechanic and World of Science and Art*

Few of those who daily pass Sir Edwin Landseer's lions in Trafalgar Square know that not far beneath their feet…in the Pleistocene gravels there are bones of the cave-lion (Felis leo spelaea).

Golden Atlas Lions from the Regent's Park Zoological Gardens were the models for Sir Edwin Landseer's famous Trafalgar Square bronze sculptures, but curiously enough, in the 1830's excavations of the foundations of Trafalgar Square numerous fossil bones of extinct prehistoric animals were unearthed. Among them were those of the original "British Lion" (*Felis leo spelaea*) and prehistoric ancestor of the Atlas Lion (*Felis leo leo*). In *The Living Age* (1887), Littell further reported that medieval Londoners had earlier discovered "the fossil bones of cave lions…[which] have lain so securely stored for untold ages beneath Charing Cross and Trafalgar Square…[but] were long known as dragon bones."

Atlas or Barbary Lions have had a long historical association with British monarchy. Captive Atlas Lions were kept in the Tower of London as early as the 12th century during the reign of Henry II and Richard the Lionheart. Two Barbary Lion skulls unearthed during excavations of the Tower were radio-carbon dated during the time of Edward I (c. 1300) and Henry V (c. 1420), respectively.

At the time of the Trafalgar Square excavations in the 1830's, the Duke of Wellington had the Atlas Lions kept in cramped cages in the Tower removed to more humane enclosures in London's Regent's Park, where Sir Edwin Landseer came to view them in 1858. One famous Victorian pure-bred Barbary Lion named Sultan lived in the London Zoo until 1896.

Alfred Edward Pease – 1899
*African Game,* Algeria

The North African Lion has today become so rare that it may be said to be nearing extinction. It lingers only in the country that might be described as the Mediterranean littoral zone, though an occasional lion is shot in the interior. Before the French came, the Turks had encouraged the Arabs to destroy them by freeing the two great lion-hunting tribes, the Ouled Meloul and Ouled Cessi, from all taxes and paying liberally for their skins. The French gave 50 francs for a skin. There are now a few lions still in the Province de Constantine, in the thick Atlas forests between Soukarras and La Calle.

Alfred Edward Pease's prediction only took a couple of decades to realize. This remnant population was ruthlessly extinguished within the next two decades. The last wild Barbary Golden Lion was shot in the remote forests of the Atlas Mountains in Morocco in 1922.

Remarkably, the Barbary Golden Lion was not the first Lion to become extinct on the African continent in modern times. It was another distinctive subspecies at the other end of the animal's range in South Africa. This was the Cape Black-Mane Lion (*Panthera leo melanochaitus*) which was almost as large as the Barbary Lion. It also exhibited a black mane as large and luxuriant as the gold mane of its cousin. Captive animals of this race were exhibited live in Amsterdam, where they may be found in the drawings of Rembrandt. The last Black-Mane Lion in the Cape was shot in 1858, while a small number survived to the north in Natal for a few more years. The last recorded sighting of this Lion was a large male hunted down in Natal and shot by General Bisset in 1865.

By 1900, the only surviving non-sub-Saharan race, the once numerous Asiatic or Persian Lion (*Panthera leo persica*) – so famously portrayed in art since Biblical times – survived only because the Nawab of Junagadh gave the beast a sanctuary in India's Gir Forest. By 1908, it was claimed there was only a single pride of 13 Lions remaining in this preserve. Fortunately, a great deal of effort has recently been made to save this subspecies and there are now several hundred Asiatic Lions in existence.

# THE LION'S GATE

### Atlas Golden Lion – 1920

At the gate was the god of Lions
Cut in a single massive stone
And raised above the desert sand

In the time of empires
This Lion's eye was a brilliant swastika
A sunwheel on the desert wind
His voice was a stone
Rolling over the roof of the world

Even the great parapet of his head
Is broken now
The foundation of the temple
Is cracked and wasted

Upon the wall
The carved images are all but gone:

Vanished men pursue vanished beasts
In that ancient dream of a green
And fruitful land

# THE SEA ELEPHANT

# STELLER'S SEA COW – 1768 – *Hydrodamalis gigas*

Georg Wilhelm Steller – 1741
## *Journal of a Voyage with Bering from Kamchatka to America*

Their capture was affected by a large iron hook, the point of which resembled the fluke of an anchor, the other end being fastened by means of an iron ring to a very long stout rope, held by thirty men on shore. A strong sailor took this hook and with five other men stepped into the boat, and one of them taking the rudder, the other four rowing, quietly hurried towards the herd. The harpooner stood in the bow of the boat with the hook in his hand and struck as soon as he was near enough to do so, whereupon the men on shore, grasping the other end of the rope, pulled the desperately resisting animal laboriously toward them. Those in the boat, however, made the animal fast by means of another rope and wore it out by continuous blows, until tired and completely motionless, it was attacked with bayonets, knives and other weapons and pulled up on the land. Immense slices were cut from the still living animal, but all it did was shake its tail furiously and make such resistance with its forelimbs that big strips of cuticle were torn off. In addition it breathed heavily, as if sighing. From the wounds in the back the blood spurted upward like a fountain.

Georg Wilhelm Steller was the only trained naturalist ever to see this animal alive. And Steller's accounts were of the first-ever encounter in the very brief bloody history of human-sea cow relations, as the animal became extinct just twenty-six years later. The only species of its genera and family, the Steller Sea Cow was distantly related to the two other surviving (but endangered) *Sirendae*: the Dugongs and the Manatees. With a maximum weight of over seven tons, it was 14 times the size of a Manatee: the marine equivalent of a full-size African Elephant. Indeed, "Sea Elephant" would have been a far more appropriate name, as both the Elephant and the Sea Cow were descended from a common prehistoric land-dwelling ancestor.

Steller was the ship's naturalist on the famous expedition of the Danish explorer Vitus Bering. During the summer of 1741, Bering sailed eastward from Kamchatka to Alaska. On the return voyage, they were shipwrecked on the desolate island that now carries Bering's name.

Georg Wilhelm Steller – 1741
*Journal of a Voyage with Bering from Kamchatka to America*

When an animal was caught with the hook, those nearest in the herd began to stir also and feel the urge to bring succour. To this end some tried to upset the boat with their backs, while others pressed down the rope and endeavoured to break it, or strove to remove the hook from the wound by blows of their tail, in which they actually succeeded several times.... It is most remarkable proof of their conjugal affection, that the male, after having tried with all his might, although in vain, to free the female caught by the hook, and in spite of the beating we gave him, nevertheless followed her to the shore, and that several times, even after she was dead, he shot unexpectedly up to her like a speeding arrow. Early the next morning, when we came to cut up the meat and bring it in the dugout, we found the male again standing by the female, and the same I observed once more on the third day when I went there by myself for the sole purpose of examining the intestines.

The Bering Expedition ship, the *St. Peter*, ran aground and was wrecked while attempting to find safe anchorage on Bering Island. A total of 32 crewmen did not survive the winter, including Vitus Bering himself. Georg Wilhelm Steller was the only officer healthy enough to take command and assumed leadership over the ten crew members not crippled by illness. Steller doctored the rest and oversaw the building of shelters and the rebuilding of the wrecked *St. Peter*. Somehow, he also managed time to record the amazing assortment of wildlife on the island that had never before been seen by man.

Among the many species discovered by Bering was this massive sea mammal which proved to be the primary food source for the survivors of the *St. Peter*. As Steller observed, the Sea Cow was their salvation: "This great beast is 28 to 35 feet long and 22 feet thick about mid-section.... Each Sea Cow provided more than seven thousand pounds of meat and fat, and the red flesh tasted much like good beef.... All of us who had partaken of it, soon found out what a salutary food it was, as we soon felt a marked improvement in strength and health."

Georg Wilhelm Steller – 1741
*Journal of a Voyage with Bering from Kamchatka to America*

These animals love shallow and sandy places along the seashore, but they spend their time more particularly about the mouths of the gullies and brooks, the rushing fresh water of which always attracts them in herds. They keep the half-grown and young in front of them when pasturing, and are very careful to guard them in the rear and on the sides when travelling, always keeping them in the middle of the herd.... In the spring they mate like human beings, particularly towards evening when the sea is calm. Before they come together many amorous preludes take place. The female, constantly followed by the male swims leisurely to and fro eluding him with many gyrations and meanderings, until, impatient of further delay, she turns on her back as if exhausted and coerced, whereupon the male, rushing violently upon her, pays tribute of his passion, and both give themselves over in mutual embrace.

Despite the hardships of survival on the island, Steller took time to closely observe the nature and habits of the Sea Cows and many other species. After eight months wintering on Bering Island, Steller and his crew built a new craft from the wrecked *St. Peter* and in August 1742 sailed back to Kamchatka with news of their discovery. This rapidly resulted in Russian exploitation and monopoly of the whole Northwest Pacific coast of Alaska – especially in the enormously lucrative trade in fur-bearing sea mammals – for over a century.

However, instead of being rewarded for his heroic efforts in bringing the survivors of the *St. Peter* safely home, and bringing the momentous news of the discovery of Alaska, Steller found himself embroiled in disputes with the petty jealousies of corrupt Russian officials and bureaucrats in Kamchatka for the next four years. Worn out by a series of arrests, trials and imprisonments, in November 1756, Steller died of fever at age 37. His *Journals* and his *De Bestiis Marinis* (*On the Beasts of the Sea*) were published posthumously in St. Petersburg, establishing him as one of the greatest naturalists of his time.

Besides Steller's Sea Cow, five other species carry the name of this extraordinary naturalist: Steller's Sea Lion (*Eumetopius jubatus*), the largest species of sea lion; Steller's Sea Eagle (*Haliaeetus pelagicus*), the world's heaviest eagle; Steller's Eider (*Polysticta sterlleri*), the smallest form of Sea Duck; the Steller's Jay (*Cyanocitta stelleri*); and the Steller's Spectacled Cormorant (*Phalacrocorax perspicillatus*), a large flightless bird that sadly suffered the same fate as Steller's Sea Cow and became extinct in 1850.

Petr Yakovlev – 1764
*Chancellery Report,* **Bering Island, Kamchatka**

From 1743 until 1763, hardly a winter passed without one or more parties spending eight or nine months hunting fur animals on Bering Island, during which time the crews lived almost exclusively on the meat of the sea cow. But that was not all, for more than half of the expeditions which wintered there did so for the express purpose of laying in stores of sea cow meat for the further journey, which usually lasted two to three years more. From 1763 the visits to Bering Island seem to grow scarcer, probably due to the very fact that sea cows had now become so nearly exterminated that the few left were insufficient to maintain any wintering and foraging expeditions.

The Russian mining engineer Petr Yakovlev wintered on Bering Island in 1754-1755. Displaying an unusually astute awareness of the severe environmental damage being inflicted on this newly discovered island, Yakovlev prophetically anticipated the extinction of the Sea Cow if over-exploitation of the species was allowed to continue. As he recorded, because of the animal's sheer size, it was estimated that four animals were critically wounded and abandoned for every one that was successfully beached and killed for food. Petr Yakovlev unsuccessfully petitioned Kamchatkan authorities and requested a *ukase* or edict from the Bol'sheretsk Chancellery prohibiting – or at least limiting – the wholesale slaughter of this species. This appeal fell upon deaf ears and the last Sea Cow was killed around 1768 on Bering Island.

# SIREN SONG

### Steller's Sea Cow – 1768

Some still nights
On the shores of Bering's sea
You may imagine them

Huge as the hull
Of an overturned ship
Moaning in the rolling surf

Fountain of hot blood pulsing
Furnace of the deep heart
Wave-worn giants, idle lovers
On the swell of the sea

Bigger than elephants
Skin like the bark of an ancient oak
Snorting like horses
Pawing the kelp meadows
With their tough hooves
Like bulls in pasture

Tide riders, storm biders
Slow to lust as elephants
Passionate as whales

Beauty here in a thing not itself beautiful
As delight in the play of light
On a mountain or a great rock
Yet something vastly alive
As these once were alive

Some still nights
On the shores of Bering's sea
You may imagine them

The great breath-song
Through the sighing night

# THE TERROR BIRD

## GIANT MOA – 1850 – *Dinornis maximus*

Joel S. Polack – 1838
### *History of New Zealand*

Among the Maori there were traditions of supernatural beings in the form of birds, having waylaid native travellers, among the forest wilds, vanquishing them with an overpowering strength, killing and devouring them. The traditions are reported with an air of belief that carries conviction.

New Zealand was an island-world that was a time-capsule of the planet forty million years ago. It was a world inhabited primarily by birds; except for bats, there were no mammals (not even marsupials) in New Zealand until the legendary arrival of the Great Fleet of the Polynesian Maoris, about 1300 AD. The first European to "discover" these islands was Dutch explorer Abel Tasman in 1642, who named it after the small island of Zealand in Holland. However, the extreme hostility of the warlike Maoris prevented further incursions by Europeans until the arrival of Captain James Cook's ship *Endeavour* in 1769. Three years later, a French expedition arrived in the Bay of Islands, but rapidly withdrew after the Maoris killed and ate 27 of its officers and men. Among those suffering this fate was the expedition's commander, Captain Marc-Joseph Marion du Fresne, after whom Mauritius' Marion's Tortoise was named.

Although both the British and French expeditions recorded hundreds of new species, the Giant Moas were not among them. Joel S. Polack's account is the first published acknowledgement of the existence of these giant birds. Polack was a trader in New Zealand between 1834 and 1837. In 1838, Polack published his two-volume *History of New Zealand*, in which he said he had found bones of a large ostrich-like bird, and added that the Maori claimed that in times not long past "very large birds existed, but the scarcity of animal food, as well as the easy method of entrapping them, has caused their extermination."

SECOND WATCH / 1 P.M. / SEXT

Reverend William Williams – 1839
*Williams' Journal*, Cloudy Bay, New Zealand

The natives there had mentioned to an Englishman of a whaling party that there was a bird of extraordinary size to be seen only at night on the side of a hill near there; and that he, with the native and a second Englishman, went to the spot; that after waiting some time they saw the creature at some little distance, which they describe as being fourteen or sixteen feet high. One of the men proposed to go nearer and shoot, but his companion was so exceedingly terrified, or perhaps both of them, that they were satisfied with looking at him, when in a little time he took alarm and strode up the mountain.

The Reverend William Williams was a Protestant missionary to the Bay of Islands in New Zealand who had translated the New Testament into Maori. Williams also compiled a Maori-English dictionary and built the first church in Poverty Bay. In the summer of 1838, Williams spent many months travelling in the East Cape district of the North Island (with another amateur naturalist, and printer, William Colenso) and recorded this incident near Waipapu.

In 1839 a traveller named John Rule obtained a 10-inch section of thigh bone of some huge creature in New Zealand and brought it back to Britain. He gave the bone to Richard Owen, an authority on prehistoric animals and the man who coined the word "Dinosaur." The bone was so massive that it looked like an ox's thigh bone. Owen initially thought this was a joke, but further examination convinced him that this was the leg bone of an unknown giant ostrich-like bird. In November 1839, Owen delivered a lecture to the Zoological Society of London in which he boldly asserted that New Zealand was once inhabited by an undiscovered species, a giant flightless bird.

Remarkably, only weeks after Owen's prophetic lecture, a shipment of Moa bones collected by the Reverend William Williams and fellow missionary the Reverend Richard Taylor reached England. These bones immediately confirmed Owen's analysis and made him famous overnight. Owen gained royal recognition and became one of the chief forces behind the creation of the British Natural History Museum at South Kensington.

William Colenso – 1842
*Journal of Natural History,* New Zealand

I heard from the natives of a certain monstrous animal; while some said it was a bird, and others a person, all agreed that it was called a Moa; and that in general appearance it somewhat resembled an immense domestic cock, with the difference, however, that if anyone ventured to approach the dwelling of this wonderful creature, he would be invariably trampled on and killed by it.

In 1841, William Colenso returned to New Zealand to search for more Moa relics. He went down the east coast of the North Island, asking Maoris to help him find evidence of these birds. He recovered five Moa thigh bones and a large number of Maori myths about these great birds and returned with them to Britain in 1842. Colenso was the first to record the name "Moa," although there is some evidence to suggest the authentic Maori name may have been "Tarepo."

In 1844, the British Governor FitzRoy spoke with an 85-year-old Maori named Haumatangi who claimed to remember the second visit of Captain Cook in 1773, and stated that the last Moa in his part of New Zealand had been seen two years before Cook's arrival. Another Maori, Kawana Papai, said he had himself taken part in Moa hunts when he was a boy about 1790. He said the birds were rounded up and killed with spears. He claimed they were dangerous to hunt, as the Moa defended itself fiercely with vigorous kicks; but as they had to stand on one leg to kick, Maori hunters would strike at the supporting leg and bring it to ground.

Excavations of other early tribal settlements have uncovered charred Moa bones and Moa eggs utilized as water bottles by native peoples. And in 1859, miners made the remarkable discovery of a Maori tomb containing a skeleton of a chieftain placed in a sitting position with its skeletal hands clutching a large Moa egg measuring 10 inches by 7 inches. Later still, in 1939 – a century after the first European acknowledgement of these semi-mythical birds – excavations by New Zealanders Roger Duff and Robert Falla in Pyramid Valley on the South Island resulted in the discovery of over 140 complete skeletons of six distinct Moa species.

Reverend Richard Taylor, M.A., F.G.S – 1855
*Te Ika A Mauri – New Zealand and Its Inhabitants*

Of all the birds that have once existed in New Zealand, by far the most remarkable is the Moa. Perhaps it is the largest bird which ever had existence, at least during the more recent period of the earth's history; and it is by no means certain that it is even now extinct! I first discovered its remains in 1839, at Tauronga, and now Waipau. These bones were of recent but undeterminable age. However, Mr Meurant, employed by the Government as Native interpreter, stated to me that in the latter end of 1823, he saw the flesh of the Moa in Molyneux harbour; since that period, he has seen feathers of the same bird in the Native's hair. They were a black or dark colour, with purple edge, having quills like those of the Albatross in size, but much coarser. He saw a Moa bone which reached four inches above his hip from the ground and as thick as his knee, with flesh and sinews upon it. The flesh looked like beef. The slaves who were from the interior, said that it was still to be found inland. A man named George Pauley, now living in Fareaux Straits told him he had seen the Moa, which he described as being an immense monster, standing about twenty feet high. He saw it near a lake in the interior. It ran from him and he also from it. He saw its footmarks before he came to the river Tairi, and the mountains.

The Reverend Richard Taylor arrived as a missionary on the East Coast and the Bay of Islands in New Zealand with the Reverend William Williams. When Taylor made the voyage to England with the manuscript of his history of New Zealand in 1855, he brought with him the Maori Chief Hoani Wiremu Hipango and gained an audience with Queen Victoria and Prince Albert.

Over the next decade, Sir Richard Owen classified, reconstructed, and named many of the Moa species. Owen gave these giant birds a scientific name to match their size: *Dinornis* or "Terror Bird" – which is comparable to his name for prehistoric reptiles: "Dinosaur" or "Terror Lizard." He named six of the dozen species now known. These were: *Dinornis robustus, D. elephantopus, D. crassus, D. giganteus* and *D. gracilis* (i.e., robust, elephant-footed, fat, giant, and slender Moa). Finally there was the *Dinornis maximus* – the Giant Moa measuring 12 to 14 feet tall and a quarter ton in weight. This was taller than the *Aepyornis maximus* of Madagascar, but at a quarter ton, only about half the weight of the Elephant Bird.

# THE EXCAVATION

### Giant Moa – 1850

The earth is pulled up like a coffin lid
Bones like unstrung bows
And a battlefield of broken spearshafts
Giant shin bones cracked
Like diviners' yarrow stalks
Beaks like shattered spearheads
The hexagrams of this dry graveyard swamp

I saw the broad clawed footprint
Of the giant bird in clay
Beneath the hump of the hill
That shadows the valley

Later we found a ring of Moa skulls
With a hunched chieftain's skeleton at its centre

Clutched in his spidery grip:
A great Moa egg
Like the dragon pearl
That is the Maori moon

Sap of the veronica wood
They called "Moa's blood"
They roasted Moa flesh on its fires
When an enemy was defiant at the death
They called him "fierce as the Moa"

And when the white man came
And the Maoris fell
When pestilence and war broke them
And all their world was ending
They cried out, "*Ka ngaro I te ngaro a te Moa*"
Alas, we are "lost as the Moa is lost"

In this valley I am shaken
By a vision rising
Like the dragon pearl moon
Eclipsing, for a dark hour
The bright noonday sun

# GALAPAGOS MUTTON

# FLOREANA ISLAND GALAPAGOS TORTOISE – 1876
## *Chelonoidis nigra nigra*

William Dampier – 1684
### *New Voyage Round the World*

The Tortoises on these Isles are so numerous that 500 or 600 men might subsist on them alone for several months without any other sort of provision. They are extraordinarily large and fat, and so sweet that no pullet eats more pleasantly. One of the largest of these creatures will weigh 150-200 lb and some of them are two foot or two foot six inches over the carapace or belly.

The Galapagos Archipelago is a group of strange volcanic islands unvisited by humans until their discovery by the Spanish in 1535. Thereafter, they were exploited for food and water by passing ships. However, for centuries they remained largely unoccupied except by adventurers and pirates who used the islands as a base for attacking Spanish treasure ships. From the end of the 17th to the middle of the 18th centuries, the Galapagos Islands served as a haven for English buccaneers like William Dampier.

Dampier must have dined upon very immature specimens of Galapagos Tortoises in his travels, unless he was describing the weight and size of the meat alone taken from these animals. Mature male Galapagos Tortoises were commonly 300 kilograms or 700 lbs in weight and females around 180 kilos or 400 lbs. The largest recorded specimens weighed in excess of 400 kilos or nearly 900 lbs and measured 1.9 metres or over six feet in length. The original Tortoise population of these islands was approximately one quarter of a million, but by 1900 this was reduced to less than 3,000 in the entire archipelago.

Dampier was the first man to sail around the world three times, and his *New Voyage Round the World* was the first round the world travelogue and sold four editions in its first two years. It made him a celebrity in British literary and intellectual circles. On 6 August 1698, John Evelyn wrote: "I dined with Mr Samuel Pepys, where was Captain Dampier, who had been a famous buccaneer, and printed a relation of his very strange adventure, and his observations. He seemed a more modest man than one would imagine by the relation of the crew he had assorted with." One of the classics of maritime writing, William Dampier's *New Voyage Round the World* was acknowledged as a great inspiration for explorers like Captain James Cook and Captain George Vancouver, as well as authors such as Daniel Defoe, Robert Louis Stevenson, and Joseph Conrad.

# SANTA FE ISLAND GALAPAGOS TORTOISE – 1890
## *Chelonoidis nigra barringtoni*

Amasa Delano – 1801
### *Voyages of Commerce and Discovery*

The Terrapin, or Land Tortoise found here is by far, the largest, best and most numerous of any place I have visited. Some of the largest weigh three or four hundred pounds; but their common size is between fifty and one hundred pounds. They have a very long neck, which, together with their head, has a very disagreeable appearance, very much resembling a large serpent. I have seen them with necks between two and three feet long, and when they saw anything new to them, or met each other, they would raise their heads as high as they could, their necks being nearly vertical, and advance with their mouths wide open, appearing to be the most spiteful of any reptile whatever. I was put in the same kind of fear that I felt at the sight or near approach of a snake when I first saw a very large one. I had a musket in my hand at the time, at the touch of the muzzle of which, he dropped himself upon the ground and instantly secured all his limbs within his shell. They are perfectly harmless, as much so as any animal I know of, notwithstanding their threatening appearance. They have not teeth, and of course they cannot bite very hard. They take their food into their mouths by the assistance of the sharp edge of the upper and under jaw, so as to nip grass, flowers, berries, or shrubbery – the only food they eat.

Amasa Delano was the Bostonian captain of the *Perseverance* who wrote of his stay in Galapagos in his *Voyages of Commerce and Discovery* (1789-1807). As Delano acknowledged, exploitation of Giant Galapagos Tortoises for food or oil was practiced by every passing ship. Today four Galapagos Land Tortoise subspecies are listed as extinct. However, recent genetic analysis has brought many classifications into dispute. It also brings into question just when a species is considered extinct. For example, the Floreana Island Tortoise definitely became extinct on Floreana Island by 1876. However, in January 2012, genetic fingerprinting of Isabella Island Tortoises revealed a number of surviving mixed-race or hybrid Floreana-Isabella Tortoises.

# FERNANDINO ISLAND GALAPAGOS TORTOISE – 1906
## *Chelonaidis nigra phantastica*

Admiral David Porter – 1812
### *A Cruise to the Pacific Coast*

Before engaging in battle, the British ship cleared her decks by heaving overboard her cargo of live elephant tortoises. A few days afterwards we were so fortunate to find ourselves surrounded by about 50 of them which we picked up and brought on board, as they had been lying in the same place where they had been thrown over, incapable of any exertion in that element, except that of stretching out their long necks.

David Porter, the Admiral of the American Pacific Fleet, reported this event in the aftermath of an engagement with a British ship in the Pacific waters north of the Galapagos during the War of 1812. In 1823, Captain Benjamin Morrel wrote an account which explains why a British man-of-war in the Pacific would take on such a large cargo of live tortoises: "I have taken many tons of these animals on board my own vessels from 5-6 months without once taking on food or water. They have been known to live unfed on some whaling ships for 14 months without any apparent diminution of health or weight."

The maximum lifespan of these Giant Land Tortoises is unknown. However, the longest-lived Pacific Galapagos Tortoise – affectionately known as "Harriet" – was a Santa Cruz Tortoise (*Chelonaidis nigra porteri*) taken from the island in 1835 by Charles Darwin. Harriet was later given to the *HMS Beagle*'s First Lieutenant John Clement Wickham and brought to Australia. Eventually, Harriet found a home in the Brisbane Botanic Gardens until her death at the age of 176 on 19 May 2006.

Strangely enough, the oldest Indian Ocean Tortoise died just one month later. This was the famous Aldabra Tortoise (*Aldabrachelys gigantean*), known as *Adwaita* (Sanskrit for the "One and Only"). Taken captive in 1750 for the menagerie of "Clive of India," One-and-Only died in the Alipore Zoo in Kolkata, India, on 23 June 2006 at the age of 250 years.

Another ancient Tortoise was the 188 year old Tonga specimen, named Tu'i Malila or "Little King." Tu'I Malila was presented to the King and Queen of Tonga by Captain James Cook in 1777. Tu'i Malila lived in Tonga's royal gardens until his death on 19 May 1965. Although considered one of the most beautiful of Tortoises, with its golden star-patterned shell, the Little King was not a giant, but a medium-sized (35 lb) Madagascar Radiated Tortoise (*Geochelone radiate*).

THIRD WATCH　2 P.M.　SEXT

# PINTA ISLAND GALAPAGOS TORTOISE – 1971
## *Chelonoidis nigra abingdoni*

Charles Darwin – 1835
### *Voyage of the Beagle*

I will first describe the habits of the tortoise, which has been so frequently alluded to. These animals are found, I believe, on all the islands of the Archipelago. The inhabitants believe these animals are absolutely deaf; certainly they do not hear a person walking close behind them. I was always amused when overtaking one of the great monsters, as it was quietly pacing along, to see how suddenly, the instant I passed, it would draw in its head and legs, and uttering a deep hiss fall to the ground with a heavy sound, as if struck dead. I frequently got on their backs, and then giving a few raps on the hinder part of their shells, they would rise up and walk away; but I found it very hard to keep my balance.

Charles Darwin found in the Galapagos a perfect natural laboratory of evolution when he visited in 1835. His observations there enabled him to put forward in *The Origin of the Species* his revolutionary theory of evolution by natural selection. Darwin wrote concerning the tortoises' immense size: "Mr Lawson, an Englishman, and vice-governor of the colony, told us that he had seen several so large, that it required six or eight men to lift them from the ground; and that some had afforded as much as two hundred pounds of meat.... The tortoises when thirsty are obliged to travel long distances. Hence broad and well-beaten paths branch off in every direction from the wells down to the sea coast; and the Spaniards by following them up, first discovered the watering-places."

The Pinta Tortoise was believed to be extinct in the early twentieth century, but one last specimen was discovered in 1971 and taken into captivity. It is now listed as "extinct in the wild" and "functionally extinct" in captivity, as no female exists. Two attempts at mating this animal with females of other subspecies have resulted in the production of hybrid eggs. However, in both cases the eggs have failed to hatch. Known as "Lonesome George," this animal is famously listed on Galapagos tourist advertisements as the "world's rarest living creature." He is estimated to be a spry and healthy one hundred years of age. He is the Galapagos Islands' most celebrated tourist attraction and lives at the Darwin Biological Research Station on Santa Cruz Island.

# LA TORTUGA NEGRA

Floreana Galapagos Tortoise – 1876

Known to the Spaniards as "*La Tortuga Negra*"
This ancient giant carefully paced out its life

Moving just fast enough to avoid the lava flow
And slow enough to endure the volcanic heat

A thousand millennia passed peacefully
As the island's lava slowly cooled in the tropic sea

Then one evening, something appeared on the horizon:
Little floating isles with lights drifted ashore

> Compare this encounter
> To the tale of Aeschylus' Turtle:
>
> A tortoise scooped up and lifted
> Into the air by an eagle
>
> From a great height – we are told
> That bird mistook the great man's bald pate
> For a large stone, and
>
> Wishing to crack open his lunch
> Let the turtle drop

Who was the more surprised, then
Upon hearing that fatal crunch:
Tortoise or Man?

One can only speculate, of course
But, most probably, with one last gasp –

> Like the last *Tortuga Negra* dropped by sailors
> Into a boiling pot –

Both died of astonishment

# THE SHOGUN'S WOLF

# SHAMANU OR JAPANESE WOLF – 1904
## *Canis lupus hodophilax*

Hirata Atsutane – 1810
### *The Superiority of the Ancients,* Japan

There are many wolves which are called the messengers of the gods of the mountains, and people from other parts of the country come and, applying through the guards of these mountains, choose and borrow one of these wolves as a defence against fire. That is to say they only arrange to borrow it and do not take a wolf to their place. And from the day of borrowing they offer daily food to the spirit of the wolf.

The Shinto shrine Mitsumine Jinga was an important site of wolf worship in Japan. By tradition it was built by Prince Yamato Takeru, the legendary unifier of Japan in the 4th century, who, during his campaign of pacification of central Honshu, became lost in the mountain passes of the Karisaka. He was rescued and guided out of the mountains by a supernatural white wolf.

The Shamanu or Yamainu (meaning "Mountain Dog") was the world's smallest wolf: weighing about 14 lbs, it measured from 12-16 inches at the shoulder, and just a little over 3 1/2 feet in length (including its one-foot-long tail). The Shamanu was endemic to the Japanese islands of Honshu, Shikoku and Kyushu.

By the Ainus, the aboriginal Japanese people, the Shamanu was called the "Howling God" because it so often howled for hours from hilltops and mountains. There is an Ainu myth origin about a white wolf that mates with a goddess; the offspring of this union became the ancestors of the Ainu.

Coenraad Jacob Temminck – 1839
*Fauna Japonica,* **Leiden, Holland**

The Shamanu or Japanese Wolf is chiefly distinguished from the European Wolf by its smaller size and shorter legs. It is as much dreaded by the Japanese as the European Wolf is in its range.

The Shamanu or Honshu Miniature Wolf was first described to Western science in 1839 as *Canis hodophilax* by Coenraad Temminck, the first director of the Dutch Museum of Natural History. This was based on specimens from the first zoological expedition to Japan by Philipp Franz von Siebold and Heinrich Burger, both Germans, employed by the Dutch at a trading post near Nagasaki.

The Shamanu was just one of several hundreds of species classified by Coenraad Temminck, twenty of which carry his name. Although there is some dispute over the matter, today the Shamanu is commonly classified as a subspecies of the Grey Wolf: *Canis lupus hodophilax.*

C.P. Hodgson – 1860
*A Residence in Nagasaki and Hakodate,* Japan

Wolves were brought to the doors of the omnivorous Europeans and offered for sale. Every Japanese house in the north had, as well as a notice giving street number and family details, a charm to keep wolves away from their doors.

Small as it was, the Shamanu seems to have been greatly feared by the Japanese. However, there was once one other indigenous wolf on the island of Hokkaido. This was the Ezo Wolf (*Canis lupis hattai*), which became extinct in Japan by 1888. It was a much larger animal than the Shamanu: heavier and longer, with a bigger head and more powerful teeth and jaws. Already rare by the mid-19th century, bounties of 7 to 10 yen ensured its extinction. Between 1878 and 1888, more than 1,500 Ezo Wolves were brought in for bounty. Since then, no sign of this animal was seen again in Japan.

N. P. Anderson – 1905

*Anderson's Report – British Zoological Expedition,* Japan

This Wolf was purchased in the flesh, and I can learn but little about it. It is rare, some say almost extinct.

N.P. Anderson was a collector for a British expedition to Japan. This skin and skull are now to be found in the British Natural History Museum in South Kensington, London. It is one of the only two or three specimens in existence outside Japan. There is a fully mounted specimen from the Fukushima Prefecture, Hondo which is preserved in the Tokyo Science Museum.

Anderson was correct about it being rare, but incorrect about it being "almost extinct." The animal killed for the British collectors on 23 January 1905, near the village of Washikaguchi, Nara Prefecture, Honshu, was the very last the world would ever see of the Shamanu: the little Howling God that was the Japanese Wolf.

# THE HOWLING GOD

Shamanu or Japanese Wolf – 1905

Broken wolf's tooth
A charm, set in pounded gold
Ancient blood in a bronze bowl

Shogun hunted Shamanu, the little wolf,
Through forests and stony fields
Horses and dogs chased him to mountains
Beneath exhausted stars

In ancient days
Legends gave him hypnotic power
Geese swooned before
The glowing of his eyes
Beneath the willow tree
Travellers and pale maidens
Succumbed to his voice

Shamanu, the little Howling God,
Ascends the Nine Heavens
Wanders the land of nine jade rivers
And nine jade mountains

Shamanu's blood is red amber now
His eye is sapphire
His flesh the cinnabar ore
That gives up bright quicksilver
And deadly vapour

# THE KANGAROO WOLF

# THYLACINE or TASMANIAN TIGER – 1936
## *Thylacinus cynocephalus*

Reverend Robert Knopwood – 1805
### *Pastor's Diary*, Risdon, Tasmania

Am engaged all the morn, upon business examining 5 prisoners that went into the bush. They informed me that on 2 May when they were in the wood they see a large Tyger that the dog they had with them went nearly up to it and when the Tyger see the men which were about 100 yards away, it went away. I make no doubt but here are many wild animals which we have not yet seen.

The name Tasmanian Tiger dates back to 1642, when the island had been "discovered" by Dutch explorer Abel Tasman who named the island Van Diemen's Land after his patron, the Governor of Batavia. That year, Francoys Jacobz, Tasman's pilot, led an expedition inland and reported "the footing of wild beasts having claws very like a tiger." Later reports by Dutch East India Company officers also mentioned "tiger" footprints. However, there were no recorded sightings until 1805.

Robert Knopwood's 18 June 1805 diary entry is the first recorded actual sighting of a Thylacine. Knopwood was the pastor for the first settlement on Tasmania: a penal colony at Derwent River founded in 1803.

The indigenous Palowi people, of Adnyamathanha Aboriginal stock, had occupied Tasmania for over ten thousand years after the end of the last ice age when the land bridge to Australia sank beneath the sea. They knew the Thylacine as the *Marrukurli* or *Inarru-kurli* and had many legends concerning the animal.

SECOND WATCH | 4 P.M. | NONE

William Oxley – 1810
*Van Diemen's Land Company Report,* Tasmania

Settlements here are free from the Native Dog – the Dingo, the dread of the Stock Holders in New South Wales. The only Animal unknown on the Continent is the Hyena Opossum, but even here is rarely seen. It flies at the approach of Man, and has not been known to do any Mischief.

In 1806, Tasmania's Deputy Surveyor-General George Harris wrote an official description of this "newly discovered" creature and assigned it a genus and species: *Dideiphis cynocephala* (or "dog-headed opossum"). He sent an illustrated report describing both the Thylacine and Tasmanian Devil to Sir Joseph Banks, President of the Royal Society and former naturalist on Captain Cook's first voyage.

The Thylacine was the world's largest carnivorous marsupial. Related to the kangaroo, it was often described as a marsupial wolf or (because of its stripes) a marsupial tiger. As it was primarily a nocturnal hunter, it also had eyes with strange elliptical pupils. Although it resembles the placental wolf, it is one of the most striking examples of "convergent evolution" – the evolution of a body shape suited to its role and resembling unrelated animals occupying similar ecological niches.

John Gould – 1863
*Mammals of Australia,* **Australia**

A price is already put upon the head of the native Tiger, as it is called; but the fastnesses of the Tasmanian rocky gullies, clothed with impenetrable forests, will, for the present, preserve it from destruction.

John Gould was Australia's greatest and most informed naturalist painter of his time; however, his confidence in the survival of the Tasmanian Tiger in remoter parts of Tasmania did not prove to be correct. Thylacines were not only given an unreasonable reputation as sheep-killers, but despite all evidence to the contrary, some settlers even revived those old European superstitions about wolves, and insisted that the Tasmanian wolf killed only for blood (both animal and human) like a vampire.

By 1820 Hobart was the second-largest town in Australia. It had shifted from whaling and sealing to a farming and sheep-ranching settlement. The Thylacine soon became a scapegoat for sheep killings, although most killings were the work of feral dogs, descendants of dogs taken· to the island in 1798.

Accounts of supposed Thylacine attacks on sheep are very dubious and were an excuse for mismanagement by the notoriously inefficient stockholders. As early as 1828 and 1829, livestock had been released into land not ready for them and without shelter. Hundreds died, compounded by unusually harsh weather in 1829. For those facing charges of incompetence, a ready scapegoat was found in the form of the Thylacine. In 1840, Van Diemen's Land Company raised the bounty to 10 shillings per head.

George Smith – 1909
*Royal Natural History Magazine,* **Australia**

The shepherds wage incessant war on the creature, in summer laying traps and hunting it with dogs, in winter following up its tracks through the snow. A reward of a pound is given for the head by the Government, but the shepherd generally rides round with the head to several sheep-owners in the district, and takes toll from them all before depositing it at the police station. In consequence a large reward must be offered for the carcass of a Tiger, and an offer of £10 during a year for a live Tiger to be delivered was unsuccessful. It pays a shepherd very much better just to hack off the head and take it round on his rides.

The year 1884 saw the setting up of local groups such as the "Buckland and Spring Bay Tiger and Eagle Extermination Society." It is unlikely that it ever existed in large numbers, but there were ridiculous stories of Thylacines hunting in packs and killing up to a hundred sheep in a night just for sport. In 1888, a bill was passed offering a £1-per-head bounty on Thylacines, a substantial amount in those days, and the animal was hunted in its own habitat far from any farms. Between 1888 and 1914 at least 2,268 Thylacines were known to have been killed and turned in. In 1910 a distemper epidemic (possibly brought in by domestic dogs) further depleted the population.

The first live captive Thylacines displayed were at Regent's Park, London in 1850. Another was displayed in a menagerie in Hobart from 1854. By the 1860s several zoos around the world had Thylacines, but they were not often seen in the wild. In 1911, London Zoo paid £68 for a single Thylacine. The last captive Thylacine in America died in the Bronx Zoo, New York, in 1919. In September 1911, the earliest film footage of a live Thylacine was made in the Beaumaris Zoo, which later became the Hobart Zoo. Here five of the seven brief silent film appearances of this animal were made: one in 1911, three in 1928 and one in 1933. The other two films were of the last living Thylacine outside of Australia in the London Zoo before its death in 1931.

H.S. Mackay – 1914
*Memoirs of a Tiger-Hunting Man,* Tasmania

A bull terrier once set upon a Wolf and bailed it up in a niche in some rocks. There the Wolf stood with its back to the wall, turning its head from side to side, checking the terrier as it tried to butt in from alternate and opposite directions. Finally the dog came in close and the Wolf gave one sharp, fox-like bite, tearing a piece of the dog's skull clean off, and it fell with the brain protruding, dead.

It was risky to hunt Thylacines with dogs; the creatures had no fear of them, and the dogs were often unwilling to tackle a trapped Thylacine, even if they outnumbered it. Even when cornered by the largest kangaroo-hunting hounds, they seemed to show little fear, and many of these valuable dogs were killed when attempting to chase them down. Thylacines could defend themselves well enough against dogs, but were no match for bullets, snares or poison. Strangely enough, there are no accounts of any even moderately successful attacks on humans, even when cornered or trapped. Despite its harmlessness to humans, the Thylacine none the less suffered the same persecution as the wolf suffered throughout the world.

Sir Ray Lankester in *Harmsworth Natural History* (1910) wrote: "When one watches the Tasmanian Wolf, one comes to the conclusion that its appearance, ways and movements suggest the fancy that it is a Kangaroo Masquerading as a Wolf, though not very successfully."

R. Boswell – 1937
*Australian Museum Magazine,* **Australia**

The former range of the Tasmanian Tiger must have been very great as I know of one Tasmanian, who with his brothers, killed as many as twenty-four of these animals during one day, and received a reward of £1 per head for each animal. Fortunately, the Tasmanian Tiger is now wholly Protected.

The last authenticated shooting of a Thylacine in the wild was on 13th May 1930 by Wilf Batty on his farm in the Mawbanna district. The last one captured was in 1933, and kept in the Hobart Zoo. This animal was filmed by David Fleay in 1933, who argued forcefully for the animal to be kept in a better facility. This animal can be seen opening its formidable gaping jaws to about a 140 degree angle.

The Tasmanian government gave the Thylacine full legal protection on 14 July 1936. While a committee considered further methods of protection, another government department was still issuing hunting permits. Two months later, on 2 September 1936, the last Thylacine in existence, the animal filmed by David Fleay and named "Benjamin" – died as the result of near-starvation and neglect in the Hobart Zoo. Absurdly, that year the image of two rampant Thylacines were placed on the official Tasmanian Coat of Arms.

Arthur Mee – 1947
*The Children's Encyclopedia,* **London, England**

A sort of nightmare wolf: its home is Tasmania, its lair is a dark cave or cleft in the rocks; its habits are those of our own wolves, reinforced with an acid tincture of peculiar savagery. It seems to be the Caliban of the wolf tribe, making up in ferocity and blank savagery what it lacks in refined cunning like other marsupials. It carries its young in a pouch, and the whimper of young Hopeful in that furry cradle has sounded in the ears of many a sheep as it has fallen a helpless victim to the fangs of the mother.

Arthur Mee perpetuated the misinformation about the supposedly bloodthirsty, sheep-killing Thylacine in his *Children's Encyclopedia.* This is from an edition circa 1946. Over a decade after the animal became extinct, the myth of this supposedly ferocious vampire-like killer persisted.

The same year, there was a recording of a popular ballad about Tasmania with a verse that conjured up the bloodthirsty image of the Tasmanian Tiger that was published in O'Lochlainn's *Folk Songs of Ireland:*

> Our cots we fence with firing
> And slumber while we can
> To keep the wolves and tigers from us
> In Van Dieman's Land.

Ironically, in 1966, Tasmanian officials declared a huge game reserve as an area of preservation for the Thylacine, which had not been seen for 30 years. A number of expeditions have been launched, but it is now agreed the Tasmanian Thylacine is extinct.

As for the original human population of Tasmania: the last of the Palowi tribal aboriginal people were hunted down and exterminated within forty years of the 1803 colonization. In the 1840's the last Tasmanians were housed by missionaries in the original convict colony buildings at Derwent River. Thirty years later, Trugenaner (Truganini), the last full-blood Tasmanian, died there in 1876.

# THE NIGHT STALKER

Thylacine or Tasmanian Tiger – 1936

1.

*Tasmanian Tiger, Kangaroo Wolf*
*Pouched Dog, Hyena Opossum*

No name seemed to fit
This creature of the night

> Head and teeth of a wolf
> Eyes and stripes of a tiger
> Gaping jaws of a crocodile

> It had the torso of a hyena
> The backward pouch of an opossum

> Front legs of a dog
> Hind legs and tail of a kangaroo

Resorting to the Lego-language
Of the ancient Greeks

We came up with *"Thylacine"*
Which is "a pouched something"

Shy and elusive
Never a danger to man

Yet, somehow we made it
A nightmare beast

2.

Still struggling toward definition,
We gave it a second Greek name:

*"Cynocephalus"* or "Dog-head"
Like a pagan underworld god

The creature didn't know
It was a chimera

Thought it was just itself
Not a composite riddling beast
Some kind of sphinx

In a land of the kangaroo and platypus
Who could say what was strange?

In fact, in its own dreamtime
We were the nightmare


3.

In this creature's world
What was truly monstrous

What was absolutely deadly
Was us

For all the First Tasmanians
Both men and beasts

Nothing so strange
Had entered their world
Since the end of the ages of ice

Nothing so sudden
And dangerous
Since the beginning

When molten fire poured down
From the night sky into the boiling sea

# THE TIGER'S TALE

## BALI TIGER – 1937 – *Panthera tigris balica*

Pliny the Elder – 65 AD
### *Natural History,* Rome

Hyrcania and India produce the Tiger, an animal of tremendous swiftness and ferocity. The late Emperor Augustus was the first person who exhibited at Rome a Tiger in the arena. This was in the consulship of Quintus Tubero and Fabius Maximus, at the dedication of the theatre of Marcellius, on the fourth day before the nones of May: the late Emperor Claudius exhibited four at one time.

Augustus Caesar's introduction of the first Tigers into the Roman arena is also mentioned by Suetonius in his *Life of Augustus*; while Lampridius informs us that the mad teenage Emperor Heliogabalus yoked Tigers to his chariot in imitation of the god Bacchus. Martial, who lived a little after Pliny, speaks of Tigers in considerable numbers exhibited in Rome by Domitian.

Christian Brothers – 1150 AD
*The Book of Beasts,* **Cambridge**

Tigris the Tiger gets his name from his rapid pace for the Persians, Greeks and Medes used to call the arrow 'tygris'. The beast can be distinguished by his manifold markings, by his courage and by his wonderful velocity. And after him the River Tigris is named because it is the swiftest of all rivers.

This description is from the Cambridge *Book of Beasts* (1150 AD), one of the many famous Latin bestiaries which were medieval books of natural (and supernatural) history. In large part, they were encyclopaedic gleanings from classical authors like Lucretius and Pliny combined with traveller's tales and folklore. This *Book of Beasts* was translated from the Latin by T.H. White, the medievalist and author of the Arthurian novel *The Once and Future King*. White's translation begins with a quotation by T.H. Huxley which perhaps explains something of the bestiary's eternal appeal: "Ancient traditions, when tested by severe processes of modern investigation, commonly enough fade away into mere dreams; but it is singular how often the dream turns out to have been a half-waking one, presaging a reality."

Baron Oscar Vojnick – 1911
## *On the East India Group of Islands,* Bali

In the western part of Bali Island, along the northern shore, in the mountains of Groendoel, we discovered tiger footprints. On November 2nd while collecting twigs to be used for the construction of a fence around the traps, the carcass of a freshly killed kidang [roe deer] was encountered by our people. The trap was set in front of the kidang in the thicket. Minaut was almost certain that the tiger would be caught in another day. I was much less convinced, as the many human tracks could have warned the tiger. But no, it came in to feed, and the trap caught one of its forelegs, just below the wrist.

In 1912, Ernst Schwarz was able to write in *Big Game Hunting* that the Tiger was "fairly common in Bali." Two decades later it was gone. The Bali Tiger was the smallest of eight subspecies of Tigers, and the first to become extinct. Today, three (Bali, Java, Casplan) of the eight subspecies of Tiger are extinct, and another four are critically endangered. The Tiger had survived millennia of hunting by man with impunity, but when modern high-powered rifles became widespread, Tiger populations rapidly declined to near extirpation everywhere.

THIRD WATCH / 5 P.M. / NONE

Arthur de Carlo Sowerby – 1923
**"China's Fur Trade," China Journal, Hong Kong**

The Tiger is the most dreaded and highly prized of the carnivores. Not only is his skin of value, but his whole carcass; for the Chinese believe that the bones, blood, heart and even the flesh of the tiger have medicinal properties of rare power, and will pay a goodly price for concoctions brewed by the apothecary that contain such ingredients as powdered tiger's knee-cap, or clotted tiger's blood. The heart of the tiger is supposed to impart to the consumer the courage and strength of the tiger itself. On this account the tiger has been hunted till he is almost extinct.

Sir James Frazer in *The Golden Bough* in 1920 wrote concerning Tiger fetishes: "The Miris of Assam prize tiger's flesh as food for men; it gives them strength and courage. But 'it is not suited for women; it would make them too strong-minded'. In Korea the bones of tigers fetch a higher price than those of leopards as a means of inspiring courage. A Chinaman in Seoul bought and ate a whole tiger to make himself brave and fierce."

George Jennison – 1928
*Noah's Cargo,* Java

The Rampoc, or 'Tiger fight' waged against men, is a Court ceremonial in which the Royal bodyguard, in four ranks and armed with long pikes forms a square of fifty yards, in the centre of which the tiger cage is deposited covered with straw. The door is held in place by a rope of equally inflammable material. The Court being assembled, two officials of high rank walk in sedately to the sound of music, fire the straw, and return equally composedly back to the ranks that open to receive them. Meanwhile, the tiger, maddened by burns and fear, is bounding frantically in the cage until the door falls, when it is sure to leave at once. Outside it may, and often does, hesitate; it looks round for a foe on which to vent its fury, and dashes, as a rule, for the two men whose isolation marks them for attack. It is received on the spears, and not uncommonly is impaled by its own leap and weight.

The second smallest species, the Javan Tiger (*Panthera tigris sondaica*), was also hunted to extinction some time around 1988. Curiously, it was on Java's Trini Island that one of the oldest human skeletal remains was discovered in 1891: the famous 700,000 year old Java Man (*Pithecanthropus erectus/Homo erectus*). It was also here, just over a century later, that the oldest Tiger skeletal remains were discovered: the 1,200,000 year old Trini Tiger (*Panthera tigris trinilensis*).

THIRD WATCH 5 P.M. NONE

VOS Company Report – 1931
*Dutch East Indian Company Survey,* Bali

In Bali the Tiger is one of the five traditional totemic Barong dancers: Tiger, Boar, Dragon, Elephant and Lion. Each represents an area of Bali that has its own protective spirit modelled on a different animal. Barong is the King of Spirits and the leader of this host of good spirits. Barong is in mortal combat with the Rangda Witch of Black Magic and her evil graveyard spirits. Despite being numbered among the protective spirits, the Tigers of Bali have enjoyed no popular protection in return. A few of this race yet live in West Bali but are having a hard time. They are much sought after by hunters from Java, so they will certainly disappear within a few years.

This Dutch East Indies Survey reported that uncontrolled hunting by Dutch colonial trophy hunters on excursions from Java was rife and fashionable. The report's prediction of extinction proved correct: the last known Bali Tiger was a female shot at Sumbar Kima in West Bali on 27 September 1937.

The third Tiger extinction was an animal over twice the size of the Bali and Java subspecies. The Caspian Tiger (*Panthera tigris virgata*) measured over 10 feet in length and weighed in excess of 500 pounds. A government and military policy of tiger eradication in Russia, combined with uncontrolled hunting in the Caspian regions of Turkey, Iran and Afghanistan, so depleted the population by the 1940's, that there were thought to be only a dozen left in the mountains of northern Iran by the late 1950s. Sometime between 1960 and 1980, the Caspian Tiger became extinct.

With the exception of the Indian Tiger (*Panthera tigris tigris*) in protected reserves in India, all other surviving tiger subspecies are critically endangered and number only in the hundreds in the wild. These are the Siberian Tiger (*Panthera tigris altaica*), the Chinese Tiger (*Panthera tigris amoyensis*), the Sumatran Tiger (*Panthera tigris sumatrae*) and the Indo-Chinese Tiger (*Panthera tigris corbetti*).

# LAST RITES

## Bali Tiger – 1937

The little prince of tigers
Is dead

The chime of temple bells
An army of votive arrows is offered
A long rope of prayer tethers the sun

Master of the emerald forest
Lord of the crystal waterfall
That feeds the sacred lake
Dread foe of the Monkey King
And the Dragon Master

He was like a flame in the forest
His fearful laughter was in the land

Now he is the small flickering light
Of an altar candle
The yellow tallow of memory
Slowly flowing away

# VIKINGS AND GAREFOWL

# GREAT AUK OR GAREFOWL – 1844
## *Alca (Pinguinus) impennis*

Jacques Cartier – 1534
### *Journals of Jacques Cartier,* Isle of Birds, Newfoundland

Some of these birds are as large as geese, being black and white with a beak like a crow's. They are always in the water, not being able to fly in the air, inasmuch as they have only small wings about the size of half one's hand, yet they move as quickly along the water as other birds fly through the air. And these birds are so fat that it is marvellous. In less than an hour we filled two boats full of them, as if they had been stones, so that besides them which we did eat fresh, each of our ships did powder and salt five or six barrels of them.

Jacques Cartier's account of this unequal meeting of Great Auk and Man on the Isle of Birds (Funk Island) off the coast of Newfoundland in 1534 is the first written record of Europeans hunting these birds in North America: "And on the twenty-first of the said month of May we set forth from this [Catalina] harbour with a west wind, and sailed north, northeast of Cape Bonavista as far as the Isle of Birds, which island was completely surrounded and encompassed by a cordon of loose ice, split up into cakes. In spite of this belt of ice our two long-boats were sent off to the island to procure some of the birds, whose numbers are so great as to be incredible, unless one has seen them; for although the island is about a league in circumference, it is so exceedingly full that one would think they had been stowed there. In the air and round about are an hundred times as many more as on the island itself."

A curious theory links the Great Auk with the discovery of North America. It proposes that the Icelandic Vikings, already familiar with Auks and aware in a general sense of bird migrations, would have noticed the seasonal disappearances and departures of vast rafts of birds in their western waters. It would have been a small step for the Vikings to conclude that these Garefowl were travelling to other, similar islands in the west. Consequently, it has been suggested they could have followed the migrating legions of Auks, who would have led them first to Iceland, and later to Newfoundland and Labrador.

The Great Auk was the strongest and swiftest of northern swimming and diving birds, and almost immune to marine predators; while its rocky nesting sites in the rough North Atlantic were for millions of years inaccessible to men. It numbered in the tens of millions until recent historic times.

Anthonie Parkhurst – 1578
*Hakluyt's Voyages,* Isle of Penguins, Newfoundland

There are sea Gulls, Murres, Duckes, wild Geese, and many other kind of birdes store, too long to write, especially on one island named Penguin, where we may drive them on a planke into our ship as many as shall take her. These birds are also called, Penguins and cannot flie; there is more meate in one of these then in a goose; the Frenchmen that fish neere the grand baie, doe bring small store of flesh with them, but victuall themselves always with these birdes.

Cartier's "Isle of Birds" of 1534, Parkhurst's "Isle of Penguins" of 1578, and Cartwright's "Funk Island" in 1792 are one and the same rookery visited by all three voyagers, and by countless others over nearly three centuries. The summer – the nesting season – was the only time that Great Auks could be taken, for the rest of the year they dispersed and lived at sea, where they were safe from human hunters. So each summer, the men came to their rookeries and set up camps where they waited for the birds to come to them. Stone corrals were constructed on the islets, and the birds were driven into them and slaughtered.

Slaying the Auks during the nesting season compounded the destruction; as did egg collection, as each nesting pair only produced a single egg. This slaughter and depredation continued unabated for nearly three centuries. The general presumption of most observers was summed up in one hunter's account written in 1622: "God made the innocence of so poor a creature to become such an admirable instrument for the sustentation of man."

By the Vikings, this bird was known as the *Geirfugl.* And by the Irish it was known as *Gearrabhul* – meaning "the strong stout bird with the spot" – which was corrupted through usage to "Garefowl." Among the Welsh, who once hunted the bird on islets off Britain's shores, they were called *Pingouins*, which means "white head." The Great Auk was the original "Penguin:" the "penguins" of the southern hemisphere having derived their name from British explorers who presumed these flightless Antarctic birds were a southern variety of the North Atlantic bird.

George Cartwright – 1792
*Journal of Transactions and Events*, **Funk Island, Newfoundland**

Innumerable flocks of sea-fowl breed upon this isle every summer, which are of great service to the poor inhabitants of Fogo when the water is smooth, they make their shallop fast to the shore, lay their gang-boards from the gunwale of the boat to the rocks, and then drive as many penguins on board, as she will hold: for, the wings of those birds being short, they cannot fly, nor escape. The birds which people bring thence, they salt and eat, in lieu of salt pork.

Fishermen and Newfoundland colonists flocked to these rookeries every nesting season to kill birds and steal eggs. Also, many new industrial uses were found for these birds: feather beds, meat for bait, oil for lighting lamps, oil for fuel for stoves, and collar bones for fish hooks; and dried Auks (full of oil) were used as torches. The annual wholesale gathering of eggs was an especially destructive practice. Just one vessel commanded by a Captain Mood took 100,000 eggs in a single day.

By 1810 Funk Island was the only West Atlantic rookery left, and these constant summer raids by oil and feather merchants' crews soon finished off even this last vast North American nesting site as well. The only place Great Auks existed after Funk Island rookery's demise was a group of islands on the southwestern tip of Iceland. Most Auks withdrew to a lonely outcropping of rock called Geirfuglasker, or "Auk Rocks" – which was a lonely and dangerous outcropping of rock so rugged, it was safe from all but the most determined and foolhardy of hunters.

In 1830, the already near-extinct species suffered a further cataclysmic disaster. A volcano erupted under the sea near Iceland and caused a seaquake that resulted in the destruction of Geirfugl Island. The last rookery of the Great Auk sank beneath the sea, and the colony was destroyed and scattered.

It became apparent that about 60 Great Auks survived the sinking of Geirfuglasker. These birds took refuge on an even smaller and equally dangerous rocky outcrop, known as Eldey Island. It is from this last station that nearly all of the skins and eggs now found in European collections have been obtained, and during the fourteen years (1830-1844) that the Garefowl frequented this rock, one bird after another was hunted down for museum bounties, until there were just two left.

Professor A. Newton – 1861
*The Last Garefowl Hunt – 4 June 1844,* Eldey Island, Iceland

As the three men leapt from the boat and clambered up on the rocks they saw two Garefowls sitting among numberless other rock-birds, and at once gave chase. The Garefowls showed not the slightest disposition to repel the invaders, but immediately ran along under the high cliff, their heads erect, their little wings somewhat extended. They uttered no cry of alarm, and moved with their short steps, about as quickly as a man could walk. Jon Brandsson, with outstretched arms, drove one into a corner, where he soon had it fast. Sigurdr Islefsson and Ketil Ketilsson pursued the second, and the former seized it close to the edge of the rock, here risen to a precipice some fathoms high, the water being directly below it. Ketil then returned to the sloping shelf whence the birds had started, and saw an egg lying on the lava slab, which he knew to be a Garefowl's. He took it up, but finding it was broken, put it down again. All this took place in much less time than it takes to tell it.

Newton gives this account as being recorded in 1861, just 14 years after the event of the slaying of this last pair of Great Auks on the Icelandic skerry of Eldey. Another oral account confirms that Brandsson and Islefsson each killed a bird, but Ketilsson, frustrated at returning empty-handed, smashed the last intact egg with his boot. A third account, by James Wolley, was published in *Ibis* in 1861: "The capture of these two birds was effected through the efforts of an expedition of fourteen men, led by Vilhjaimur Hakonarsson; but only three were able to land on the rock, and they at great risk, namely, Sigurdr Islefsson, Ketil Ketilsson, and Jon Brandsson. Only two Great Auks were seen, and both were taken – Jon capturing one, and Sigurdr the other. It appears that this event took place between the 2nd and 5th June 1844. It appears that this expedition was undertaken at the instigation of Herr Carl Siemsen, who was anxious to obtain the specimens...the birds were sold for eighty rigsbank-dollars, or about £9."

It is notably ironic that Great Auk relics have continued to appreciate in value over the years since its extinction. In 1934, in the midst of the Depression, one stuffed Great Auk sold for nearly $5,000, or five years' wages for a fisherman; and a single egg for two years' wages. Then, on 4 March 1971, the Icelandic Natural History Museum paid £9,000 for a single mounted specimen of a Great Auk.

# ALPHA AND OMEGA

## Great Auk or Garefowl – 1844

In the year 1844, Isambard Kingdom Brunel
Stood on the iron deck of the first transatlantic passenger liner
As the age of sail gave way to the age of steam

In that year, Samuel Morse
Sent a coded message singing through the steel lines
And electric relays of America's first telegraph

Its chosen path was alongside the railway line
Between Baltimore and Washington

The message was biblical and portentous
It read: "What hath God wrought?"

In the year 1844, three daring men climbed
Up a precarious chimney of volcanic rock
In the wave lashed North Atlantic

Here the last lonely pair of Great Auks
Were chased down and slaughtered
Their last egg crushed

This too heralded the birth of our modern age
"What hath God wrought?"

# DARWIN'S DOGS

# WARRAH or ANTARCTIC WOLF-FOX – 1876
## *Disicyon australis*

Lord John Byron – 1741
### *Adventures of Midshipman John Byron,* Falkland Islands

Four creatures of great fierceness resembling wolves, ran up to their bellies in the water to attack the people in the boat and so we were forced to put out to sea again to find a safer haven further along the sandy shore. But soon as we saw the beasts again in a state of alarm we set fire to the tussock to get rid of them. But in this we had greater effect than expected as the country was ablaze as far as the eye could reach for several days, and we could see them running in great numbers.

The *Adventures of Midshipman John Byron* included the wrecking of his ship *The Wager* in the notorious Straits of Magellan. Midshipman John Byron eventually became Captain John Byron, the fourth Lord Byron and grandfather of the great Romantic poet George Gordon, the sixth Lord Byron. This was one of the most famously harrowing adventures of the time. With the survivors of the wreck, John Byron arrived on the Falklands where he encountered these seemingly ferocious "Wolves." Like his grandson, Byron was a controversial character who earned the name "Foul Weather Jack" after his promotion to rank of commodore after he completed a record-breaking twenty-two month circumnavigation of the globe. As commander of the *Dolphin* and *Tamar* he claimed the Falklands for George III in 1764, despite France's Marquis de Bougainville's simultaneous efforts at colonization of those islands that same year.

Curiously, the first description of this "Wolf-Fox" on record came from Richard Simson, who sailed on the British ship *The Welfare* in 1690: "We saw foxes twice as big as in England, we caught a young one, which we kept on board for some months." However, Simson's ship became engaged in a battle in the first Falklands War in which the Wolf-Fox became the first casualty: deciding a battleship was no fit place for man or beast, the poor creature panicked after the first cannon volley and leapt overboard.

Dom Pernetty – 1764
*A Voyage to the Malouin Islands,* Falkland/Malouin Islands

Officers of M de Bougainville's suite were, so to speak, attacked by a sort of wild dog; this is, perhaps, the only savage animal and quadruped which exists on the Malouin Islands. But, perhaps too, this animal is not actually fierce, and only came to present itself and approach us, because it had never before seen men. The birds do not fly from us: they approached us as if they had been tame.

Dom Pernetty, also the author of *Dissertation Upon America,* was a member of the Marquis de Bougainville's famous expedition. These uninhabited islands in the South Atlantic were called the Malouin Islands by the French, the Malvinas by the Spanish, and the Falkland Islands by the British, and were seen by all three powers as a key safe port for ships attempting to passage from the Atlantic to the Pacific.

The Marquis Louis-Antoine de Bougainville also described this animal and its habits in his *Voyage Round the World* (1770): "The Wolf-Fox, so called, because it digs itself in earth and because its tail is longer and more fully furnished than that of a wolf, lives in the dunes of the sea shore. It follows the game and plans its trails intelligently, always by the shortest route from one bay to another. On our first landing we quite believed that they were the paths of human inhabitants."

The Marquis de Bougainville's historic circumnavigation of the globe in 1766-69 in the frigate *La Boudeuse* and the store-ship *L'Etoile* just preceded Captain James Cook's first voyage in the *HMS Endeavour* to the South Pacific, where both men were ordered to observe the transit of Venus in 1778. Bougainville's was only the 20th circumnavigation of the world since Magellan's 250 years previously, in 1519, and since the second by Sir Francis Drake 190 years before, in 1580. It was also the first circumnavigation by the French, and the first that could be said to have a true "natural science" agenda.

Charles Darwin – 1833
## *Zoology of the Voyage of the Beagle,* Falkland Islands

Their numbers have been greatly decreased by the singular facility with which they are destroyed. I was assured by several of the Spanish countymen, who are employed in hunting cattle which run wild on these islands, that they have repeatedly killed them by means of a knife held in one hand and a piece of meat to tempt them to approach in the other. The number of these animals during the past fifty years must have been greatly reduced: already they are entirely banished from half of East Falkland. It cannot, I think, be doubted, that as these islands are now being colonized, before the paper is decayed on which this animal is figured, it will be ranked among those species which have perished from the earth.

Charles Darwin, while on the islands, observed the "Falkland Island Wolf-Fox" or "Antarctic Wolf" (that was locally known as the Warrah) and collected three skins, two of which were later presented to the London Zoological Society. What interested Darwin most about the Warrah was that it was the only predator on the islands and, apart from a small variety of mouse, the only land mammal. The Warrah seemed to live on an unlikely diet of mice, sea birds, eggs, and (perhaps) small sea mammals.

Just how the Warrah could have evolved on these isolated islands without any substantial prey species, and with no other related species on the islands at all, was something of a mystery to Darwin. As Darwin's prophecy of extinction quite rapidly came to pass, the mystery of the Warrah's evolution is not likely to be resolved.

Lt. Colonel Charles Hamilton-Smith – 1839
*The Dog Tribe,* **Edinburgh**

The Falkland Island Aquara Dog I discovered in the fur stores of Mr Jacob Astor in New York, a large collection of peltry which came from the Falkland Islands, where, according to reports that gentleman received, his hunters had nearly extirpated the species.

Artist-naturalist-antiquarian-spy, Hamilton-Smith, a veteran of the Napoleonic and 1812-14 Wars, was the author of many books on natural history and an authority on the history of military uniforms and costumes. He was only slightly incorrect, in that the Astor hunters did not quite extirpate the "Antarctic Wolf-Fox" or "Aquara Dog." A few stragglers hid out in the hills for another few decades, and remarkably enough, in 1868 one captive Warrah was acquired by the London Zoo in Regent's Park. There it survived for a number of years, narrowly missing out on being the last of its species. That dubious honour was bestowed upon a wild Warrah at Shallow Bay in the Falkland's Hill Cove Canyon, where it was shot and skinned in 1876.

The first North American wolf to become extinct was the Newfoundland White Wolf in 1911. This animal's scientific name was *Canis lupus beothucus* in ironic recognition of the similarly extinct Beothuk Indians of Newfoundland. Other North American wolves exterminated during the 20th century were the Kenai Wolf (*Canis lupus alces*) of the Kenai Peninsula in Alaska in 1915; the Texas Grey Wolf (*Canis lupus monstrabilis*) and the New Mexican Mogollon Mountain Wolf (*Canis lupus mogollonensis*), both in 1920; the Great Plains Lobo Wolf (*Canis lupus nubilus*) in 1926; the Southern Rocky Mountain Wolf (*Canis lupus youngi*) in 1940; and the Cascade Mountains Brown Wolf (*Canis lupus fuscus*) in 1950.

Besides these lost North American forms of *Canis lupus* (Grey Wolf), all three forms of *Canis rufus* (Red Wolf) became extinct in the wild (or so interbred with coyotes as to cease to exist as a pure species) by 1980. These were: the Texas Red Wolf (*Canis rufus rufus*), the Mississippi Red Wolf (*Canis rufus gregoryi*), and the Florida Black Wolf (*Canis rufus floridanis*).

# WARRAH'S LAST SONG

### Warrah or Antarctic Wolf-Fox – 1876

Everybody heard singing in the night

One went to the valley to listen
One climbed the hill to see

A wolf was sitting far off
On a high ridge beneath the stars

He was singing
He was an old wolf
His teeth worn and broken

He was an old wolf
On a high ridge beneath the stars

He was an old wolf
But he sang a young wolf's song

> *At daybreak I go*
> *At daybreak I go I run I go*
> *At daybreak I go I run I go*
> *At daybreak I go*

He was an old wolf
On a high ridge beneath the stars

He was an old wolf
But he sang a young wolf's song

> *At daybreak I go*
> *At daybreak I go I go I go*

# COLUMBUS' CURLEWS

## ESKIMO CURLEW – 1985 – *Numenius Borealis*

Christopher Columbus – 1492
### De Las Cassas, *Columbus' Journal,* Sargasso Sea

Immense flocks of birds, far more than we have seen before, passed overhead all day long, coming always from the north and heading always towards the southwest. Which led the admiral to believe that they were going to sleep on land or were, perhaps, flying from the winter which was about to come to the lands from which they came. On this account the admiral decided to abandon the westward course and to steer west-south-west, with resolve to proceed in that direction for two days but after two days, more birds were sighted and all that night his men heard birds passing so for two days again they sailed west-south-west, whereupon the Pinta being the swifter ship went on ahead of the Santa Maria and was the first to sight land.

> In 1961, the ornithologist James Tooke wrote: "*Columbus' Journal* tells us the birds the sailors snared from these immense flocks were plainly field birds that could not possibly find rest on water.... Consequently, Columbus decided to change course and follow the birds in hope of finding land. Five days later, Columbus set foot on the island of San Salvador.... Although the mariners did not know what the non-stop birds were, the date and direction of flight – at that time and in that place – identify them as Eskimo curlews and golden plovers, making their oversea flight one of 2,500 miles."

John James Audubon – 1833
*Ornithological Biography*, **Labrador**

During a thick fog, the Esquimaux Curlews made their appearance near the harbour of Bras d'Or. They evidently came from the north, and arrived in such dense flocks as to remind me of the Passenger Pigeons. They continued to arrive for several days, in flocks which seemed to me to increase in number. They flew in close masses, sometimes high, at other times low, but always with remarkable speed, and performing beautiful evolutions in the air. The appearance of man did not intimidate them, for they would alight so near us, or pass over our heads at so short a distance, that we easily shot them.

The legendary John James Audubon was America's greatest pioneering ornithologist and artist. Born Jean-Jacques Fougère Audubon in Haiti, he was the illegitimate son of a French naval officer and privateer, and a Spanish Creole mistress from Louisiana. The Haiti 1788 slave rebellion forced Audubon's father to return to France, where the boy was raised and educated. To avoid conscription in the Napoleonic Wars, the young Audubon travelled to America on a false passport where he became a frontiersman and merchant. Eventually he settled on his life's passion as an ornithologist and wildlife artist. He was a trailblazer in his portrayal of life-size birds "drawn from life," and in publishing *Birds of America* with its magnificent octavo colour plates, which was subscribed to by 1100 patrons and earned him $36,000.

The Eskimo Curlew was one of the champion long-distance migrants: flying from the shores of the Arctic Ocean and the Bering Sea to Labrador and the Gulf of St. Lawrence, then making a 4,000 kilometre non-stop ocean crossing to Guiana and Brazil, then overland to southern Argentina and Chile – and as far south as Tierra del Fuego. The return route was up the Pacific side of South and Central America before reaching Texas and Nebraska, and northward back to the High Arctic in an enormous elliptical loop over the entire North and South American continents. This was an overall migratory flight of over 30,000 km.

Dr. A.S. Packard – 1861
*Ornithological Journals,* Labrador

The Curlews appeared in great numbers. We saw a flock a mile long and nearly as broad; the sum total of their notes sounded at times like the wind whistling through the rigging of a thousand ton vessel; at others the sound seemed like the jingling of multitudes of sleigh-bells.

The noted Massachusetts ornithologist Edward Howe Forbush, author of *Birds of New England,* first observed vast flocks of Passenger Pigeons as a child in the 1860's. When he wrote about them in 1916, he explained the manner of their demise: "When the Passenger Pigeon began to decrease in numbers, about 1880, the marksmen looked about for something to take its place in the market in the spring. They found a new supply in the great quantities of Plover and Curlews in the Mississippi valley that season.... They were shot largely for western markets at first; they began to come into the eastern markets in numbers about 1886.... These markets were: Halifax, Montreal, Philadelphia, Boston, New York, Wichita, St. Louis, Chicago and Detroit. Boston shipments alone amounted to tens of thousands of birds every spring through 1887 to 1896."

Myron H. Swenk – 1915
*Procedures of the Nebraska Ornithologists Union*

In the 1880's, hunters would drive out from Omaha and shoot until the slaughtered birds literally filled wagonloads up with the sideboards on. Sometimes when the flight was unusually heavy and the hunters were well supplied with ammunition their wagons were too quickly and easily filled, so whole loads of the birds would be dumped on the prairie, their bodies forming piles as large as a couple of tons of coal where they would be allowed to rot while the hunters proceeded to refill their wagons with fresh victims.

The first president of the Nebraska Ornithologists Union, Dr. Lawrence Bruner, wrote about the Eskimo Curlew in 1896: "These flocks reminded the settlers of the flights of passenger pigeons and the curlews were given the name of 'Prairie Pigeons'. They contained thousands of individuals and would often form dense masses of birds extending for a quarter to a half mile in length and a hundred yards or more in width. When the flock would alight the birds would cover 40 or 50 acres of ground."

Myron Swenk also noted: "In the Midwest states the fields where they were known to gather were patrolled regularly and scanned with binoculars. Sometimes a gunner would put himself in a line of flight where he had only to shoot one bird from a flock to cause the remaining birds to circle again and again until most or all had been shot. He then waited for the next flock."

The vast migratory flocks of Eskimo Curlew had virtually vanished everywhere by 1900. The last birds were sighted and shot in Nebraska in 1911. The last record of the appearance of Eskimo Curlews in the state of Massachusetts was on August 28, 1929 when they appeared on a dinner table at a hotel at Schoodic Point.

The birds last seen in South America were shot in 1925. Less than a dozen sightings of individuals were recorded over the next century, and many of these have proven to be similar curlew-like species. The last confirmed sighting was in 1963. The last "possible" sightings of more than a single bird were in Texas in 1981 and Kendall Island, Northwest Territories, in 1985.

# CRY OF THE CURLEW

## Eskimo Curlew – 1985

1.

Knud Rasmussen among the Inuit
Claimed the word for poem
Was *Anertsa*, meaning "a breath"

Neither speech nor song
But fixed musical diction

A flow of beautiful smooth words
Recited in a low voice
Delivered at a moderate pace

A crystallized form of natural language
That must be worked and shaped
As smoothly and carefully as soapstone

Word images and word charms
Polished like walrus ivory

Old pieces are learned from the elders
They are passed round and admired
Like fine carvings or well-made weapons

But do not use them too often
Do not wear them out

These charms were made for protection
Against disease, against the evil effects
Of shooting stars, of cunning foes, of envy

When death occurs, strict mourning taboos
Are observed, but when the taboo is lifted

The bereaved ones use these charms
Murmuring them each to the other
And each to those now gone

2.

Rasmussen also records another Inuit word
For poem: *Taigdlia*, meaning "to name"

There have been 40 common names
For the Eskimo Curlew

One Inuit name meant "Swiftwing"
A Cree meant "Sweetgrass"
An Abnaki name meant "Beaked One"

Many other names were made
In imitation of their various cries

Among the Inuit they were called
*Pi-pi-pi-uk, Tura-Tura* and *Ak-ping-ak*

To the Cree *Wee-kee-me-nase-su,*
*Wee-kee-me-new, We-Ke-wa-ne-so*


3.

This recitation of their many names
Links them together like prayer beads on a rosary

Grants the passage of their many souls
Across that Other World's continents

In the outports of Labrador
They were the *Gallou Bird* and the *C'lew*

Among the Québécois
They were *Corbigeau des Esquimaux*
While the farmers of Ontario
Called them *Little Sicklebills*

Market hunters named them *Doughbirds*
And *Futes* in New England and New York
And *Prairie Pigeons* in the American West

The Islanders of the Caribbean greeted them
As *Wood Snipe, Chittering* and *Shivering Curlew*

While to the Latinos of Venezuela and Columbia
They were known as *Zarapito esquimal*
In Uruguay as *Chorlo polar*

And *Chorlo campino*
In the pampas of the Argentine


4.

So this poem is my word charm,
Smooth and polished as I can make it

Let us hear your names again:
Little Sicklebill, Sweetgrass, Swiftwing

And your voice carried
Like your wings on the north wind:

*Pi-pi-pi-uk, Tura-Tura*
  *Wee-kee-me-nase-su*
    *Wee-kee-me-new*
*We-Ke-wa-ne-so*

# THE GOLDEN AGE

# GIANT WHITE SWAMPHEN – 1830 – *Porphyrio albus*

Surgeon Arthur Bowes – 1788
## Ship's Log: Lady Penrhyn, Lord Howe Island, Tasman Sea

I could not help but picturing to myself the Golden Age as described by Ovid – to see Fowls and Coots and Reels walking totally fearless and unconcerned in all parts round us so we had nothing more to do than stand a minute or two and knock down as many as we pleased. If we missed them they would never run away. The Pidgeons also were as tame and would sit upon the branches till you might go and take them off with your hands. Many hundreds of all sorts together with Parrot and Paroquets, Magpies and other Birds were caught and carried on board our ship with the Charlotte.

The Lord Howe Island Giant Swamphen – also known as the White Gallinule – was just one of over a hundred species of birds that inhabited this isolated island in the Tasman Sea between New Zealand and Australia. No human had set foot on this small island (measuring five miles by one mile) and its tiny satellite islet. Indeed, its avian inhabitants had no contact with any sort of mammals (except bats) and no predators of any sort. However, everything changed on 13 March 1788, when the British ship *HMS Supply* arrived with the *Scarborough, Lady Penrhyn* and *Charlotte,* and the island was named Lord Howe, in honour of the First Lord of the Admiralty.

The red-billed, white-feathered and flightless Lord Howe Island Giant Swamphen was the largest representative of its family of "Coots and Reels" (that is: *Coots* and *Rails* of the *Rallidae* family) in Polynesia. Being large, prominent and unafraid of humans, it rapidly became the island's first and most obvious candidate for extermination. It is known from only three existing skin specimens and two illustrations. Two were made on that first encounter in 1788 by Thomas Watling and John White; and by George Raper on a second visit in 1790. The Giant White Swamphen was certainly extinct by 1830.

Captain Thomas Gilbert – 1788
*Ship's Log: Charlotte,* **Lord Howe Island, Tasman Sea**

Several of these Birds I knocked down, and their legs being broken, I placed them near me as I sat under a tree. The pain they suffered caused them to make a doleful cry which brought 5 or 6 dozen of the same kind to them and by that means I was able to take nearly the whole of them.

Early European observers never seemed to tire of their own amazement at the tameness of birds which had never before seen men. Yet their reactions to such unwariness were always predictably and brutally the same. This kind of unbridled slaughter of huge numbers of the entirely tame birds by the crews of ships which made regular stops on voyages out of Australia's Sydney Harbour resulted in the dramatic reduction of the once abundant bird populations on this small island. There were once well over a hundred bird species on the island; most were vagrant or migrating species that existed elsewhere. However, a dozen endemic species had nowhere else to go, and eight of these are now extinct; the other four are critically endangered. The Giant Swamphen in 1830, Lord Howe Island Blue Pigeon (*Columba vitiensis godmanae*) in 1853, and the Red-Fronted Green Parakeet (*Cyranoramphus novaezelandiae subflavescens*) in 1869 were the first to be exterminated.

These first ships were part of one of the world's greatest sea expeditions: the First Fleet of 11 ships that on 13 May 1787 sailed from Britain to establish the first European colony in New South Wales, Australia. A naval escort consisting of the flagship *HMS Sirius* and the armed tender *HMS Supply* accompanied six convict transport ships (including two former slave ships) and two food transport ships. The journey of over 24,000 km of the 11 ships and 1400 people travelled 252 days without loss of a ship and fewer than 70 deaths – considering the conditions – was something of a triumph of the tactical planning and navigational skills of Captain (later Admiral) Arthur Phillip. The fleet landed at Botany Bay on 18 January 1788, just 18 years after Cook's first landing; but finding this unsuited to settlement sailed into what Phillip described as "the finest harbor in the world, in which a thousand sail of the line may ride in the most perfect security." He named it Sydney Harbour in honour of the British Home Secretary, Lord Sydney. There Phillip established the first British settlement in Australia on 26 January 1788 – now annually celebrated as Australia Day.

Dr. James Foulis – 1847
*Resident's Journal,* **Lord Howe Island, Tasman Sea**

There are but few birds that belong to this island – the only valuable kind being a large pigeon.

For half a century, Lord Howe Island was a stopping-over place on the journey between Sydney and Norfolk Island. It also was used by whalers for water and food. A small settlement of three men with Maori wives and two children was established in 1834, subsisting on trade with passing ships. In 1851, during Dr. James Foulis' stay on the island, there was a population of only sixteen colonists.

Just how vulnerable flightless birds can be to human incursion was dramatically demonstrated by the case of New Zealand's Stewart Island Wren (*Xenicus [Traversia] lyalli*). At the northern tip of New Zealand's South Island, the one mile square wooded Stephens Island had a human population of exactly one. The following is a British Ornithological Society Report published in 1895: "At a recent meeting of the Ornithologist's Club in London, the Hon. W. Rothschild, the well-known collector, described this veritable rara avis, specimens of which he had obtained from Mr Henry Travers of Wellington, who, we understand, got them from the lighthouse-keeper at Stephens Island, who in his turn is reported to have been indebted to his cat for this remarkable ornithological 'find'. As to how many specimens Mr Travers, the lighthouse-keeper and the cat managed to secure between them we have no information, but there is very good reason to believe that the bird is no longer to be found on the island, and as it is not known to exist anywhere else, it has apparently become quite extinct. This is probably a record performance in the way of extermination. The English scientific world will hear almost simultaneously of its discovery and its disappearance."

Another endemic New Zealand bird species was also rapidly extinguished in an equally arbitrary manner. The Huia (*Heteralocha acutirostris*) was a totally unique and beautiful bird with long black and white tail feathers which were traditionally only worn by Maori Chiefs. A hat with Huia feathers was presented to the future George V of England on a royal visit in 1900. The result was an immediate European craze for Huia feathers. A brief seven years later, in 1907, the Huia was declared extinct. In 2010, a single Huia feather sold at auction for NZ $8,000.

Alan McCulloch – 1921
*Birds of Lord Howe Island,* Tasman Sea

This paradise of birds has become a wilderness and the quietness of death reigns where all once was melody. The very few birds remaining are driven from their nests by rats, and their eggs eaten.

The June 1918 grounding of the *SS Makambo* at Ned's Beach allowed black rats onto the island previously protected by an anchorage which only allowed landing by small boats. With the wreck of the *Makambo*, the last pockets of the island's endemic bird populations – already critically endangered through hunting and habitat destruction from humans and introduced goats, pigs and cats – suffered their final fatal blow. Within 2 to 7 years, the Doctor Bird or L.H.I. Vinous-tinted Blackbird (*Turdus xanthopus vinitinctus*) in 1920, the L.H.I. Big Grinnel Flycatcher (*Gerygone igata insularis*) in 1920, the L.H.I. White Eye (*Zosterops strenua*) in 1923, the Rainbird or L.H.I. Fantail Warbler (*Ripidura fuliginosa cervina*) in 1924, and the L.H.I. Red-Eye Starling (*Aplonis fuscus hullianus*) in 1925 – all joined the Swamphen, Green Parakeet and Blue Pigeon on the list of extinct species from this tiny island.

As mentioned, the remarkable Giant White Swamphen was a member of the *Rallidae* family, which has a 70 million year old ancestral line, and consists of Rails, Crakes, Coots and Gallinules: the order *Gruiformes*, which include Bustards and Cranes. This order is largely made up of ground-feeding, ground-nesting, walking birds that rarely fly, and many are today critically endangered: especially on remote Pacific isles. Besides the Lord Howe Island Giant Swamphen, at least ten other Pacific Island Rails are known to have become extinct: the Chatham Island Modest Rail (*Gallirallus modestus* – 1900), Chatham Island Dieffenbach's Rail (*Gallirallus dieffenbachia* – 1840), Macquarie Island Banded Rail (*Gallirallus philippensis macquariensis* – 1880), Fiji Barred-Winged Rail (*Nesoclopeus poeciloptera* – 1965), Tahiti Rail (*Gallirallus ecuadata* – 1900), Samoan Wood Rail (*Pareudiastus pacificus* – 1873), Carolina Island Kittlitz's Rail (*Porzana monasa* – 1850), Iwo Jima Rail (*Poliolimnas cinereus brevipes* – 1924), Laysan Island Rail (*Porzana palmeri* – 1944), and the Wake Island Rail (*Gallirallus wakensis* – 1945).

Introduced cats, pigs, goats and rats were frequently the reasons for the final extinction of Rail species on small islands. The Laysan Island Rail suffered a similar fate to the birds of Lord Howe Island when during the Second World War a wrecked American landing craft drifted ashore and black rats escaped onto the island. The Wake Island Rail also failed to survive the war, not because of rats, but rather gruesomely because a besieged garrison of starving Japanese soldiers hunted down and ate the entire population.

# OVID'S ISLAND

### Giant White Swamphen – 1830

*"It was in the murderous age of iron*
*That men spread sails before the wind*
*And came to live on plunder"*

So it was on the Tasman Sea
When the convict ships came to this isle
Where no man had ever trod before

These iron men swiftly brought an end
To the last earthly relic of Ovid's fragile *Age of Gold*

*"And the quietness of death reigns*
*Where once was melody"*

Here the pale ghost of the whistling Swamphen
Stalks the pandanus groves and palm glades

And the shades of the Rain Bird and the Fantail
The Doctor Bird, the White Eye and the Red-Eye Starling

And those many others who no longer sing
Upon the branches of the flowering white cedar

Nor tremble as the sea wind blows upon the petals
Of the wedding lily or the mountain rose

# THE FEATHERED GODS

# HAWAIIAN OAHU O-O – 1837 – *Moho apicalis*

Captain James Cook – 1779
### *The Third Voyage of Captain James Cook,* Hawaii

The islanders have another dress appropriated to their Chiefs, and used on ceremonious occasions, consisting of a yellow feathered cloak and helmet, which, in point of beauty and magnificence, is perhaps nearly equal to that of any nation in the world. These feathered cloaks are made of different lengths, in proportion to the rank of the wearer, some of them reaching no lower than the middle, others trailing on the ground. The inferior Chiefs have also a short cloak, resembling the former, made of the long tail-feathers of the cock, the tropic and man of war birds, with a border of the small red and yellow feathers, and a collar of the same. Others again are made of feathers entirely white, with variegated borders. These feathered dresses seem to be exceedingly scarce, appropriated to persons of the highest rank, and worn by the men only.

Lt. James King of the *HMS Discovery* later added to this account with a passage describing Cook's welcome by the Hawaiians in Kealakekua Bay on 26 January 1779: "The next day, about noon, the king, in a large canoe, attended by two others, set out from the village in great state. Their appearance was grand and magnificent. In the first canoe was Terreeoboo and his chiefs, dressed in their richest feathered cloaks and helmets, and armed with long spears, and daggers; in the second, came the venerable Kaoo, the chief of the priests, and his brethren, with their idols displayed on red cloth. These Idols were busts of gigantic size, made of wicker-work, and curiously covered in the small feathers of various colours, wrought in the same manner with their cloaks. Their eyes were of large pearl oysters.... As soon as I saw them approaching, I ordered out our little guard to receive the king; and Captain Cook...arrived nearly at the same time...when the king rose up, and in a very graceful manner threw over the Captain's shoulders the cloak he himself wore, put a feathered helmet upon his head, and a curious fan in his hand. He also spread at his feet five or six other cloaks, all exceedingly beautiful, and of the greatest value."

The magnificent feathered cloaks and helmets that were presented to Captain Cook were eventually brought to Britain and are still held as part of the British Museum's collection. And as Captain Cook himself recorded: "A more rich and elegant Dress than this perhaps the Arts of Europe have not yet been able to supply."

## MOLOKAI O-O – 1904 – *Moho bishopi*

Captain George Vancouver – 1794
### *'The Discovery' Journal of Captain George Vancouver,* Hawaii

King Kamehameha was garbed in a striking yellow cloak made principally of bright yellow feathers which reached from his shoulders to the bottom of the canoe. On his head he wore a very handsome feathered helmet, and made altogether a magnificent appearance.

The cloak of King Kamehameha described by Captain George Vancouver was constructed over a period of eight generations of kings, and was believed to have been made from the plumes of over 80,000 birds. The thousands of golden plumes that made up these royal cloaks were taken almost entirely from the four O-O species (*Moho apicalis, M. bishopi, M. nobilis, M. braccata*) and the single Mamo species (*Drepanis pacifica*) – all of which are now extinct. This cloak was the feathered equivalent of the crown jewels of the Hawaiian kings. However, it doesn't appear as if this was the ultimate cause of their extinction, as it was forbidden for commoners to hunt these birds or possess their feathers except on behalf of the royal family. Also according to some accounts, many of these birds were captured and stripped of their gold plumes rather than killed.

Goats, sheep and cattle put ashore by Captain Cook and Captain Vancouver between 1778 and 1794 caused extensive damage to native forests. Subsequently, much forest has been cut down by Europeans in order to plant sugar, pineapples and coffee. Imported rats, cats and mongoose took a terrible toll on native birds, while imported domestic pigeons resulted in a plague of avian malaria that exterminated all Honeycreepers and Honeyeaters below 4,000 feet in altitude – which is the range of its deadly imported carrier, the Night Mosquito.

Nor were the islands' birds the only victims of the European invasions that followed Captain Cook. The native Polynesian population at the time of Cook's visit was estimated between 400,000 and 800,000. By 1900, the native population was 40,000, and by 1950 it was less than 10,000, or a decrease of 98% of their original population, and only 2% of the Hawaiian non-native population of 500,000. By 2010 it had increased to 250,000 or nearly 20% of Hawaii's 1¼ million population.

# HAWAII O-O – 1934 – *Moho nobilis*

Coenraad Jacob Temminck – 1838
*Manuel D'Ornithology,* **Leiden, Holland**

The most striking characteristic of *Moho noblis* is a tuft of beautiful long silky feathers decorating each flank; the bright yellow colour of this waving plume makes a pleasing contrast to the otherwise dark colouring of its plumage. These are the feathers Sandwich Islanders use to make their cloaks. The English traveller Dixon tells us they catch these birds with ease, pull out bunches of feathers on the flanks, and then let the birds go.

The first O-O Honeyeater to become extinct was the Oahu O-O (*Moho aplicalis*) in 1837. This was undoubtedly because Oahu was the most densely populated island and the location of the port of Honolulu. The second extinction was the related but non-Moho species, the Kioea (*Chaetoptila angustipluma*) in 1850; and the third was the Molokai O-O (*Moho bishopi*) in 1904. The Hawaiian O-O (*Moho noblis*) was the most numerous species of Hawaiian Islands Honeyeaters because its habitat on the Big Island of Hawaii was the most extensive. Because of this, it was nearly the last of the Honeyeaters to become extinct, in 1934. The only exception was a tiny population of Kuaia O-O (*Moho braccata*) which miraculously survived until 1987 in an isolated patch of forest in a high-altitude volcanic cone within the island. This was above the range of the Night Mosquito and, as the site of the world's highest recorded rainfall, of little interest to feral cats.

In 2008 DNA analysis revealed that Hawaiian Honeyeaters did not evolve from Australasian Honeyeaters (*Meliphagidae*), and that they belonged to the entirely distinct family of Mohoidae, consisting of two genera and five species. This is the only known extinction of an entire avian family in historic times.

SECOND WATCH / 10 P.M. \ COMPLINE

# KAUAI O-O – 1987 – *Moho braccata*

J.C. Greenway – 1967
*Extinct and Vanishing Birds of the World,* New York

Five forms of the Honeyeater family – known as the O-O – were once to be found on as many of the Hawaiian Islands. These were all strikingly beautiful, either brown or jet black, with metallic reflections and with bright yellow ornamental plumes. All of these are now extinct. Because the natives captured them for their yellow plumes it has often been said that they were extirpated by the Hawaiians, but it is not probable that this was the cause of their disappearance. As in the case of the extinction of twenty forms of the Hawaiian Honeycreepers, it is probable that destruction of the native forests is the primary cause.

Honeycreepers were the youngest of all bird families and among the most beautiful and varied. All descended from one ancestor species that a century ago had evolved into 9 genera, twenty-two species and sixty-four subspecies. All measured from 10 to 21 cm and were brilliantly coloured with specialized beak forms for feeding on flowering trees.

Ninety-seven percent of all Hawaiian plant and tree species are endemic and unique to the islands. By 1950, three quarters of the natural forests were lost to cultivation, cattle browsing or fire. Over 270 plant species, subspecies and varieties are known to be extinct and 800 more are endangered. In fact, an astonishing sixty percent of the 68 known forms of native land birds are probably extinct.

As noted, all five endemic Hawaiian Honeyeaters are now extinct; and forty percent of all endemic Hawaiian Honeycreepers are also gone. These include: the Mamo (*Drepanis pacifica*), Black Mamo (*Drepanis funereal*), Ula-Ai-Hawane (*Ciridops anna*), Laysan Apapane (*Himatione sanguinea freethi*), Great Amakihi (*Loxops sagittiriostris*), Molokai Alauwahio (*Loxops maculata flammea*), Lanai Alauwahio (*Loxops maculate montana*), Oahu Akepa (*Loxops coccinea rufa*) Hawaiian Akiola (*Hemingnathus obscurus obscurus*), Lanai Akiola (*Hemingnathus obscurus lanaiesis*), Oahu Akiola (*Hemingnathus obscurus ellisianus*), Kauai Akiola (*Hemingnathus obscurus procerus*), Oahu Nukupuu (*Hemingnathus lucidus lucidus*), Kauai Nukupuu (*Hemingnathus lucidus hanapepe*), Maui Nukupuu (*Hemingnathus lucidus affinis*), Greater Koa Finch (*Psittirostra palmeri*), Lesser Koa Finch (*Psittirostra flaviceps*), and Kona Finch (*Psittirostra kona*).

# THE ANCESTORS

### Hawaiian Oahu O-O – 1837

The Ancestors prepare to sail
They raise the mast of the outrigger
And pray to Kanaloa
For a calm sea and swift passage

As a fair wind rises, the Ancestors
Depart for the isle of the Feathered Gods

Where still the lush Koa forests bloom
And the winged jewel-and-gem birds
Sing to the glory of flowering trees

Where fly the O-O and the Mamo
Whose whirring wings are fashioned
Of glittering gold and the sheen of jet

Where they feed on the honey flower
With the emerald Amakihi
And the ruby bright Alauwahio

And others with plumes the colour
Of citrine, tourmaline, amethyst and pearl

Flit through forests heavy with flower and fruit
Filled with bird song and sunlight

# THE VAN DYKE

# IVORY-BILLED WOODPECKER – 1951 – *Campephilus principalis*

Mark Cateby – 1731
*Natural History of Carolina, Florida and Bahama Islands*

The Bill is white as Ivory, three inches long, and channelled from basis to the point: the Iris of the eye is yellow: the hind-part of the Head adorned with a large peaked crest of scarlet-feathers: a crooked stripe runs from the eye on each side the Neck, towards the Wing: the lower part of the Back and Wings (except the large Quill-feathers) are white, all the rest of the Bird is black. The Bills of these Birds are much valued by the *Canada Indians,* who make coronets of them for their Princes and great warriors by fixing them round a Wreath, with their points outward. The *Northern Indians,* having none of these Birds in their cold country purchase them from the Southern people at the price of two, and sometimes three buck-skins a bill.

The Ivory-billed Woodpecker was always a rather rare bird. As early as 1785, the Welsh naturalist Thomas Pennant reported that the bird was "scarce." Its territory was broad but it was very specialized and thinly populated. Before the heyday of the timber industry (1800-1900) the Ivory-bill inhabited all mature low-lying timberland in south-eastern North America. It needed considerable tracts of mature timberland to be able to find sufficient food to live on; each breeding pair would cover a territory of more than 2000 acres. And with their conspicuous markings and loud, resonant calls these red-crested birds were once relatively easy to find in their habitats.

The pre-eminent pioneer of American natural history of the time was the English artist-naturalist Mark Cateby with his landmark *Natural History of Carolina, Florida and Bahama Islands: Containing the Figures of Birds, Beasts, Fishes, Serpents, Insects and Plants.* Nearly a century before Audubon, Cateby was the first naturalist to create folio-size colour engraved plates.

Cateby was the first ornithologist to publish a description of this bird which he called the "Large White-Billed Woodpecker," but he mentions that "the Spaniards call 'em Carpentaros" because of their rapid destruction of wood. It is best known as the Ivory-billed Woodpecker, but over the years became known by a variety of other names: Pearl Bill or Pearly-billed Woodpecker, King Woodpecker, Log-Cock, King Wood Cock, and Lord God Bird. In Louisiana, the Cajun French knew the bird as *Grand pique-bois, Poule de bois,* and *Grand Pic Noir a bec blanc.*

Alexander Wilson – 1812
*American Ornithology*, **North Carolina**

I had secured a wounded specimen of this remarkable bird and saw no harm in keeping it for a short time in my hotel room. In less than an hour I returned, and, on opening my door he set up a distressing shout, which appeared to proceed from grief that he had been discovered in his attempt to escape. He had mounted along the side of the window, nearly as high as the ceiling, a little below which he began to break through. The bed was covered with large pieces of plaster, the lath was exposed for at least fifteen inches square, and a hole large enough to admit a fist, opened to the weatherboards; so that, in less than another hour he would certainly have succeeded in making his way out.

Alexander Wilson was a Scottish-American poet, naturalist, illustrator – and the most important pre-Audubon figure in American ornithology. Indeed, Audubon's encounter with the older artist-naturalist in Louisville, Kentucky in 1810 may have inspired him to consider publishing his own work. Wilson began his encyclopaedic *American Ornithology* in 1805. It was published in 9 volumes from 1808 to 1814 and included 268 species. Wilson died in 1813 before the last volume could be printed.

The Ivory-billed Woodpecker was certainly the most famous of all Woodpeckers. At 20 inches (50 cm) and over one pound in weight (500 gm) it is among the most spectacular; however, it was actually only the second largest species. The largest – measuring a remarkable 23 inches (58 cm) – was the Imperial Woodpecker (*Campephilus imperialis*), which once inhabited the mature pine forests of Mexico's Sierra Madres. Similar in size to the Raven, the Imperial was nearly twice the weight of the Ivory-bill. Only one ornithologist had observed this bird while it was alive. The first specimen was acquired in 1832, and the last in 1950.

Not a single photograph of a live Imperial Woodpecker was known to exist. Astonishingly, in 2011 Cornell University released newly acquired film footage of a living Imperial Woodpecker. This remarkable vivid 16mm colour film was taken by an amateur ornithologist and dentist from Pennsylvania, named William L. Rhein. In 1956, Dr. Rhein travelled to the district of Durango in the Sierra Madres where, while riding on a mule, he spotted and filmed an adult female Imperial Woodpecker in some ancient pine trees. Dr. Rhein died in 1999, apparently unaware of the historic significance of his home movie.

John James Audubon – 1826
*Ornithological Biography*, Kentucky

I have always imagined, that in the plumage of the beautiful Ivory-billed Woodpecker, there is something very closely allied to the style of colouring of the great Van Dyke. The broad extent of its dark glossy body and tail, the large and well-defined white markings of its wings, neck and bill, relieved by the rich carmine of the pendent crest of the male, and the brilliant yellow of its eye, have never failed to remind me of some of the boldest productions of that inimitable artist's pencil. The flight of this bird is graceful in the extreme. The transit from one tree to another, even should the distance be as much as a hundred yards, is performed by a single sweep, and the bird appears as if merely swinging itself from the top of the one tree to that of the other, forming an elegantly curved line. At this moment all the beauty of the plumage is exhibited, and strikes the beholder with pleasure. Its notes are clear, loud, yet rather plaintive. They are heard at a considerable distance, perhaps half a mile, and resemble the false high note of a clarinet they are usually repeated three times in succession, and may be represented by the monosyllable *pait, pait, pait.*

John James Audubon is the third and greatest of America's pioneering ornithologist-artists. The Ivory-bill was one of his favourite subjects, and became the most sought-after and investigated of all rare birds. It has been estimated that not more than 500 Ivory-bills survived into the first half of the 20th century, yet during that time 400 traceable specimens were collected by museums: 140 in just two American museums alone. The last verified sighting of an American Ivory-billed Woodpecker was in 1951.

For a time, it seemed that the last hope for the Ivory-billed Woodpecker resided in a sole surviving subspecies: *Campephilus principalis bairdii* in Cuba. In 1960, there were theoretical estimates that a small population of twenty Cuban Ivory-billed Woodpeckers were surviving in a remote Cuban forest reserve. Sadly, by 1974, this population had vanished; but then in March of 1986, hope was again renewed with a possible sighting of a pair of birds in Cuba's Jaguani Forest Reserve. However, since that time nothing more has been reported.

President Theodore Roosevelt – 1907
*Theodore Roosevelt: An Autobiography*, **Louisiana**

In stature, in towering majesty, the Louisiana cypress are unsurpassed by any trees of our eastern forest; lordlier kings of the green-leaved world are not be found until we reach the sequoias and redwoods of the Sierras.... The most notable birds and those which most interested me were the great Ivory-billed woodpeckers. Of these I saw three, all of them in groves of giant cypress; their brilliant white bills contrasting finely with the black of their general plumage. They were noisy but wary, and they seemed to me to set off the wilderness of the swamp as much as any of the beasts of the chase.

In 1907, Theodore Roosevelt set out on a bear hunt in the ancient cypress forests (in what became known as the Singer Forest Reserve) near Tallulah, Louisiana. Roosevelt's hunting ground was the last great swath of virgin Mississippi River hardwood bottomland forest left in America – and consequently the last refuge of the nation's Ivory-billed Woodpecker. Over the next two decades there were very few sightings of a bird that many believed was extinct.

In 1935, however, seven pairs of America's rarest bird were discovered on the reserve. Then, from 1937 to 1939, James Tanner managed (at the last possible moment) to study and film a nesting pair in the reserve and produce his authoritative study *The Ivory-billed Woodpecker*. However, by 1939, the Singer population declined to just six birds, and Tanner estimated the entire population of Ivory-bills in America was not more than twenty-two birds.

After the destruction of the old growth habitat on the Singer Reserve by large scale logging operations, there was only one fully confirmed sighting of the Ivory-bill in America in 1951. However, there have been many unconfirmed sightings and a multitude of second-hand accounts throughout rural southern United States. Most of these appear to have been sightings of that other large red-headed Woodpecker, the Pileated Woodpecker (*Drocopus pileatus*).

In 2005, there was believed to be a valid sighting of the bird in the "Big Woods" Forest Reserve in Arkansas. This was followed up by video evidence of a living Ivory-billed Woodpecker. However, the video has proved to be highly controversial, and despite a massive multi-million dollar search and monitoring operation, nothing has subsequently been seen or heard of the Lord God Bird.

# THE LORD GOD BIRD

### Ivory-billed Woodpecker – 1951

Forged in the deep brilliant mind
Of some savage god

Then hidden away, in the twisting of river bends
Mazing channels, sloughs and levees

And in the swelling waters of these ancient forests
Of giant cypress, blackgum and red ash

Mohawk red crest mounted
On a flickering jackhammer head

The *"thump, thump, thump"*
Beating heart of the bayou

The swooping fiery spirit
Of this twilight world

Flame we can no longer see
Song we can no longer hear

Searching for this bird, we find
In the lost language of the Natchez
Only the word *"Pu-kup"* meaning "red"

We learn its *"yap yap yap"* call
Was followed by a plaintive cry
Like the sound of a tin horn,
Or a cracked clarinet

Now at one with the vanished
Biloxi, Muskogee and Quapaw
*"Downstream People"*

Flame we can no longer see
Song we can no longer hear

# SCREAM OF THE QUAGGA

# QUAGGA – 1883 – *Equus quagga quagga*

George Edwards – 1758
### *Gleanings of Natural History,* London

This curious animal was brought alive, together with the male, from the Cape of Good Hope: the male dying before they arrived at London, I did not see it; but this female lived several years at a house of his Royal Highness, the Prince of Wales, at Kew. The noise it made was much different from that of an ass, resembling more the confused barking of a mastiff-dog. It seemed to be savage and fierce in nature: no one would venture to approach it, and could not mount on its back. I saw it eat a large paper of tobacco, paper and all; and I was told, it would eat flesh, or any kind of food they would give it. I suppose that proceeding from necessity, or habit, in its long sea voyage; for it undoubtedly feeds naturally much as other horses and asses do, I mean on vegetables.

George Edwards was an aristocratic artist-naturalist who recorded the arrival of this first Quagga to reach Britain from the Cape of Good Hope. On the recommendation of Sir Hans Sloane, Edwards had been appointed the librarian of the Royal College of Physicians. Besides *Gleanings*, Edwards also published his earlier *History of Birds*, in which he described and illustrated more than 600 species never before described or delineated. He was later to become known as the "Father of British Ornithology."

The Quagga was often mistaken for some sort of cross-bred animal: half-zebra, half-horse. It was, in fact, a distinctive type of Zebra. Its head and forequarters were striped like a zebra while its hindquarters were a solid rufous brown. Alternatively, the Edwards animal was for a time believed to be the female variation of the fully striped white-legged Burchell's Cape Zebra. In fact, Burchell's Zebra (*Equus quagga burchelli*) is now classified as a subspecies of the nominate Quagga species (*Equus quagga quagga*) and both suffered the same fate.

Zebras from "Ethiopia" were known to the Romans when the historian Dio Casio described them as "horses of the sun resembling tigers." However, it was William Dampier, the famous adventurer and buccaneer, who, upon visiting the Dutch Colony of the Cape of Good Hope in 1691, first gave a description of Burchell's Cape Zebra: "a very beautiful sort of wild ass whose body is curiously striped with equal lists of white and black."

William John Burchell – 1811
*Travels in the Interior of Southern Africa,* London

I could compare the clatter of their hooves to nothing but to the din of a tremendous charge of cavalry, or rushing of a mighty tempest. I could not estimate the accumulated number at less than fifteen thousand, a great extent of the country being actually chequered black and white with their congregated masses. As the panic caused by the report of our rifles extended, clouds of dust hovered over them, and the long necks of troops of ostriches were also to be seen, towering above the heads of their less gigantic neighbours, and sailing past with astonishing rapidity. Groups of purple Sassaybes and brilliant red and yellow Hartebeests likewise lent aid to complete the picture, which must have been seen to be properly understood, and which beggars all attempt at description.

William John Burchell was a remarkable English explorer and naturalist who from 1810-15 gathered over 50,000 specimens in the most extensive collection of African plant and animal species ever amassed – before or since. From 1825-30, he made a similarly extraordinary collection in Brazil which included 16,000 insects, and 1,000 animals. As an authority of Southern Africa – having travelled over 7,000 kilometres of largely unexplored territory – Burchell was instrumental in the parliamentary decision in favour of British emigration to the Cape in 1820. In later years much angered by disputes with the British Museum, and feeling unappreciated after having totally exhausted his own personal fortune in creating these astounding collections, Burchell took his own life in 1863.

The "purple Sassaybes" and the "red Hartebeests" colourfully described by Burchell in his *Travels* as part of these vast herds of Quaggas and Burchell's Zebras were sadly also all hunted to extinction. *Sassaby* was the Saan Bushmen's name for a "goat-horned" antelope with a blue-grey coat that the Boers called *Blaauwbok* and the English called Blue Buck (*Hippotragus leucophaeus*). Burchell's "red Hartebeest" was the nominate Cape Red Hartebeest (*Alcelaphus caama caama*).

The remarkable and unique Blue Buck was actually the first African animal to become extinct in historic times: the last specimen being shot about eighty years after its discovery by Europeans in 1799. By the 1830's, all of the Cape Red Hartebeest herds had been reduced to a handful of animals that were kept in a private reserve until they too were killed off by poachers by 1940.

Jared Diamond – 1997
*Guns, Germs, and Steel,* New York

"Efforts at domestication of zebras went as far as hitching them to carts: they were tried out as draft animals in 19th century South Africa. Alas zebras become impossibly dangerous as they grow older. Zebras have the unpleasant habit of biting a person and not letting go. They thereby injure even more American zoo-keepers each year than do tigers. Zebras are also virtually impossible to lasso with a rope because of their unfailing ability to watch the rope noose fly toward them and then to duck their head out of the way. Hence it has rarely (if ever) been possible to saddle or ride a zebra, and South Africans' enthusiasm for their domestication waned."

In England in the 1830's there was a brief vogue for Quaggas as harness animals after Sheriff Parkins became famous in London society for his pair of exotic imports. A few decades later, Lord Rothschild rode in a carriage pulled by two Burchell's Zebras. Eventually, however, both the Quagga and the Zebra proved to be too unpredictable. Quaggas in particular were prone to dangerous fits of rage. In 1860, the Regent's Park Zoo's only attempt to breed captive Quaggas failed when the stallion beat itself to death in its enclosure.

The last wild Quagga stallion was hunted down in the Cape in 1878; and the last captive Quagga died in the Artis Magistra Zoo in Amsterdam on the 12 August 1883. Only 23 specimens of the Quagga now exist in museums anywhere in the world.

Burchell's Zebra, known to the Boers as the *Bontequagga* (meaning "painted Quagga"), managed to avoid extinction for a few decades longer than its cousin. The last known Bontequagga died in captivity in London's Regent's Park Zoo in 1910.

FIRST WATCH | 12 P.M. | MIDNIGHT

# HORSES OF THE SUN

## Quagga – 1883

1.

Bushmen called them *Quay-Hay*
In imitation of their "barking neigh"

Memories of them gather like thunderclouds
On the edge of this landscape of the mind:

A high veldt with kloofs and koppies
Where thoughts like strong winds gust

Through the tall grass, acacia
Whistling thorn and quiver trees


2.

Knowing they have no concept of heaven
Or hell or soul or resurrection
I summon them anyway

And for a moment, the gates are forced
By the rolling thunder of thousands
Upon thousands of pounding hooves

Legions of stallions and mares
Burst onto the veldt

>   *"Horses of the sun resembling tigers"*
>   According to Dio Cassio

>   Nostrils flared, *"savage and fierce by nature"*
>   Magnificent in their defiance

While the Boer hunters wait
Over water with long guns

3.

The Orion constellation
Is read differently here

Still the Celestial Hunter
But the sword is no sword
This one carries a spear

    And the three stars
    Of the belt are no belt

    But three Quagga
    The hunter's prey

For millennia after stars have gone out
We still marvel at the beauty of their light

The brilliant memory of what once was

# XENOPHON'S ONAGERS

# ASSYRIAN ONAGER – 1930 – *Equus hemionus hemippus*

Xenophon – 401 BC
## *Anabasis: The March of Cyrus,* Mesopotamia

Cyrus now advanced through Arabia, having the Euphrates on the right, five days' march through the desert, a distance of thirty-five parasangs. In this region the ground was entirely a plain, level as the sea. There were wild animals, however, of various kinds; the most numerous were wild asses; there were also many ostriches, as well as bustards and antelopes; and these animals the horsemen of the army sometimes hunted. The wild asses, when any one pursued them, would start forward a considerable distance, and then stand still; and again, when the horse approached, they did the same; it was impossible to catch them, unless the horsemen, stationing themselves at intervals, kept up the pursuit with a succession of horses. The flesh of those that were taken resembled venison, but more tender.

Travelling through Mesopotamia in 1884, Canon Tristram wrote of the Assyrian Onager: "This is the Wild Ass of Scripture and the Ninevite sculptures mentioned by Strabo, Eratosthenes, Artemidorus, Homer, and Pliny. Measuring just one metre at the shoulder, it was the smallest and swiftest of all the horse family."

Xenophon's adventures are among the most famous in all of military history. He commanded an elite force of ten thousand Greek mercenary soldiers who supported Cyrus, a pretender to the throne of the Persian Empire. The Greeks completely routed the opposing army, but disastrously Cyrus was killed in the battle, so Xenophon's Greeks had to fight their way over thousands of miles back to Greece.

Xenophon's observations were precisely confirmed over twenty-two centuries later by the British explorer Blandford in 1876: "It is said the Onager can not be caught by a single horseman in the open. But at other times they are caught in relays of horsemen and greyhounds. Some say their meat is prized above all other venison."

SECOND WATCH   1 A.M.   MIDNIGHT

Sir Austen Layard – 1850
*Nineveh and Its Remains,* **Mesopotamia**

A great herd of Wild Asses are seen in the Sinjar region west of Mosul. Those mentioned by Xenophon must have been seen in these very plains. The Arabs sometimes catch the foals during the spring, and bring them up with milk in their tents. They are of light fawn colour – almost pink. The Arabs still eat their flesh.

Sir Austen Layard's remarkable travels to Mesopotamia were made expressly to uncover the lost civilizations of Assyria. He succeeded in discovering the lost cities of Nineveh and Nimrod, and the palaces of Ashurbanipal and Sennacherib. It was his knowledge of Xenophon and the Scriptures that led to his success. Here, while camped on the desolate site of ancient Nineveh, Layard remembers the biblical passages relating to wrath of Jehovah being unleashed upon Sennacherib and quotes Zephaniah (ii,13-15): "And He will stretch out His Hand against the north, and destroy Assyria; and will make Nineveh a desolation, dry like a wilderness...a place for beasts to lie down in": an accurate description of Assyria's fate.

J.E.T. Aitchison – 1885
**British Botanical Expedition, Persia**

My guide took me to a slight elevation, above the 'Plain of Wild Asses'. For some time I could see nothing; at last whilst using my glasses, I noticed clouds of dust, like a line of smoke left in the track of steamers. These several lines of dust-cloud were caused by herds of Asses, galloping in various directions over the great plain. One herd came well within a mile's distance; from its extent, I am even now of the opinion that the herd consisted of at least 1000 animals. I counted sixteen of these lines of dust-cloud at one time on the horizon.

J.E.T. Aitchison conducted botanical surveys of Persia and Afghanistan for the Royal Botanical Gardens at Kew for Sir William Hooker. Wild Asses are of two distinct types: the African Wild Ass (*Equus africanus*), ancestor of the domestic donkey, and the irascible and never domesticated Asian Onager (*Equus hemionus*). Besides the Assyrian Onager of Syria and Mesopotamia there was one other subspecies in the Near East: the Persian Onager (*Equus hemionus onager*) – now critically endangered with only about 500 animals in two reserves in Iran. Aitchison's account testifies to the immense numbers that, before the introduction of modern firearms, once inhabited these now nearly empty deserts.

SECOND WATCH   1 A.M.   MIDNIGHT

William Ridgeway – 1905
*Contributions to the Study of Equidae,* London

That the Onager was regularly captured and domesticated in Assyria in ancient times is clearly established by one of the bas-reliefs discovered by Sir Austen Layard at Nineveh. The relief, which is one of a series of slabs recording scenes in the life and hunting expeditions of Ashurbanipal (668-626 BC), represents two of the king's attendants lassoing a wild ass. The other two asses are seen running away.

William Ridgeway is correct here. Sir Austen Layard was not only aware that he was following in the footsteps of Xenophon, but interestingly enough, this is the same animal Layard discovered precisely observed by a sculptor over 2400 years earlier in the royal hunt on the walls of Nineveh that he was in the process of excavating. And furthermore, besides the Onager, there are found the images of the Persian Lion and the Aurochs – all three suffering the same fate as the Assyrians.

Austen Layard later presented the British Museum – along with these massive relief wall sculptures of the royal hunt portraying the Assyrian Onager – a specimen of this same species: the only wild-caught example in any British collection.

This region of Old Mesopotamia between the Tigris and the Euphrates rivers has been the setting for many other military adventures for over five thousand years. It has seen the rise and fall of the Sumerians, the Babylonians, the Hittites, the Assyrians, the Medes, the Persians, the Greeks, the Romans, the Mongols, the Turks, and the British. And Mosul seems to have been the seat of power for extravagantly ruthless dictators from the days of Sennacherib to those of Saddam Hussein.

Otto Antonius – 1938
*On the Recent Equidae,* Vienna

The little Hemippus of Mesopotamia and Syria, domesticated by the ancient Sumers before the introduction of the horse became totally extinct in recent years. It could not resist the power of modern guns in the hands of the Anazeh and Shammar nomads, and its speed, great as it may have been, was not sufficient always to escape from the velocity of the modern motor car which more and more is replacing the Old Testament Camel-Caravan.

The social anthropologist Jared Diamond writes extensively about the how and why of the process of domestication of animals. He wonders why, out of the world's 148 possible big wild herbivorous mammal candidates – although a number have been "tamed" – only a dozen have been successfully domesticated, and only six have been universally adopted: sheep, goat, pig, cow, horse, and donkey.

Interestingly enough, Diamond points out that, while there are eight distinctive species of wild equids (horses and relatives) that would all appear to be suitable candidates, only two of them – the Tarpan as the ancestor of the Horse and the North African Ass as the ancestor of the Donkey – were successfully domesticated. He then specifically observes the case of the Assyrian Onager. "Closely related to the North African ass is the Asiatic ass, also known as the Onager. Since its homeland includes the Fertile Crescent, the cradle of Western civilization and animal domestication, ancient peoples must have experimented extensively with onagers. We know from Sumerian and later depictions that onagers were regularly hunted, as well as captured and hybridized with donkeys and horses. Some ancient depictions of horse-like animals used for riding or for pulling carts may refer to onagers. However, all writers about them, from Romans to modern zookeepers, decry their irascible temper and their nasty habit of biting people. As a result, although similar in other respects to ancestral donkeys, onagers have never been domesticated."

The last wild Assyrian Onager was shot in 1927 in Arabia, while the last captive animal died in the Schönbrunn Zoo in Vienna in 1930. This, despite the efforts of the Zoo's director Otto Antonius, one of the co-founders of modern zoological biology, and one of the leading lights in the rescue of such endangered species as the Wisent.

SECOND WATCH   1 A.M.   MIDNIGHT

# THE WALLS OF NINEVEH*

## Assyrian Onager – 1930

"Onagers are among the beasts of the royal hunt on the walls
of Ashurbanipal's palace at Nineveh." – Sir Austen Layard, 1850

1.

When those in the heavens
    Had not been named
When those beneath the earth
    Were without a name

We raced alive and free
    With no need of names
The speeding world was turning
    Beneath our bright hooves

As whirlwinds and sandstorms
    Arose in our wake
And chased the sun's fire
    Across the desert sky

2.

Then later came those Others
    With their names and words
With their dark incantations
    And even darker spells

Building kingdoms and empires
    By the power of words
With names to own and suppress
    And spells to enslave

Mastering the art of slaughter
    Made a paradise
Watered with the tears of slaves
    And the blood of beasts

3.

In these passageways of word
    And image cut in stone
In these corridors of power
    In the great king's house

With lion-slaying arrows
    With axes and spears
With horse-slaves and chariots
    The lord of the hunt reigns

Here we too are captives
    In this counterfeit world
Where we forever flee
    The king's deadly wrath

4.

When shall we come back
    From this eternal night?
When shall we come back
    To the world of light?

When shall we come back
    And these shackles sever?
When shall we come back
    To our life forever?

Then with a voice like thunder
    This dreadful wonder
Ends our soul's endeavour
    With its answer: "Never!"

* "The Walls of Nineveh" elegy is a curious literary exercise. It is an attempt at an ancient Sumerian verse stanza form. It may be the first new poem to be composed in this form in about three thousand years.

# OUT OF DREAMTIME

# TOOLACHE WALLABY – 1939 – *Wallabia greyi*

Sir Joseph Banks – 1770

## *The Endeavour Journals of Joseph Banks,* Queensland, Australia

Quadrupeds we saw but few and were able to catch few of them that we did see. The largest was calld by the natives *Kangaru*. It is different from any European and indeed any animal I have heard or read of except the Gerbua of Egypt, which is not larger than a rat when this is as large as a midling Lamb; the largest we shot weighd 84 lb. It may however be easily known from all other animals by the singular property of running or rather hopping upon only its hinder legs carrying its fore bent close to its breast; in this manner however it hops so fast that in the rocky bad ground where it is commonly found it easily beat my grey hound, who tho he was fairly started at several killd only one and that quite a young one.

Sir Joseph Banks was an aristocratic gentleman and natural scientist who, in *The Endeavour Journals of Joseph Banks*, recorded his discoveries as part of Captain James Cook's first expedition to the South Pacific. The Cook expedition was nominally a scientific one sent to observe the transit of Venus in the South Pacific, but sealed orders opened at sea revealed to Cook that his secret mission was to seek out "Terra Australis Incognita" – and claim it for the British Crown.

On 20 April 1770, Captain James Cook sighted the east coast of Australia. Landing at Botany Bay, Cook then proceeded up the east coast of the continent. His ship ran aground on the Great Barrier Reef and he had to spend seven weeks on the coast of what now is Queensland repairing the damage. It was here that Banks made an extensive collection of unique species of Australian flora and fauna, and became the first European to observe one of the many "Kangaroo" species (which includes Wallabies). The name *Gangarru* comes from the language of the Aboriginal Guugu Yimithirr people.

Banks was the President of the Royal Society for 43 years and was the intellectual force behind the settlement of Australia and the historic launching of the First Fleet of colonists, soldiers and convicts in 1787-88, less than two decades after Cook's discovery of the continent.

John Gould – 1840
*The Mammals of Australia,* Melbourne

I never saw anything so swift of foot as the Toolache Wallaby. It does not appear to hurry itself until the dogs have got pretty close, when it bounds away like an antelope with first a short jump, and then a long one, leaving the dogs far behind. One hunter complained bitterly after a week in the bush: 'I have had twenty runs a day with four swift dogs and not succeeded in getting one.' Another hunter claimed to have pursued one animal on horseback for over three miles without success.

John Gould, the artist-naturalist, was the most meticulous of Australia's 19th century wildlife illustrators. Son of a Royal Gardener at Windsor, he initially assisted his father as a taxidermist, and eventually was appointed to the Royal Zoological Society. His expedition to Australia in 1838-40 culminated in the monumental publication of his *Birds of Australia* (1840-48) in 7 volumes, and *Mammals of Australia* (1845-63) in 3 volumes. Gould became the foremost authority on Australian birds and mammals.

The Toolache Wallaby was considered by all to be the swiftest and most beautiful of all the Kangaroo family. It measured about five feet, nose to end of tail, and was highly valued both for its fur and as a game species. It was capable of speeds of over 45 mph. The Toolache Wallaby inhabited the open plains of South Australia, and favoured open ground "intersected by extensive salt lagoons and bordered by pine-ridges." Relying on its speed to outrun dingoes or aboriginal hunters, its choice of open ground made it easy prey for long range rifles of white hunters. Sadly, these skin hunters with rifles were extremely successful. The animal's magnificent skins were still being marketed in great numbers in Melbourne even in 1923 when there were only a couple of bands of a dozen left in the wild.

The Toolache or Grey's Wallaby scientific appellation *greyi* was given in honour of Sir George Grey KCB, who led two disaster-ridden expeditions into previously unexplored regions of Western Australia. He later became governor of Western Australia, then New Zealand and Cape Colony – and eventually Prime Minister of New Zealand.

Professor F. Wood Jones – 1924
*Preservation of the Toolache Wallaby,* **Robe, South Australia**

By far the fleetest of all the Wallabies, and the fairest. There cannot be more than a few score of these animals left in existence; including the 14 animals protected by Mr Brown here on the Konetta Station. And yet, the poaching continues. Their beautiful pelts have been marketed in very large numbers in the sales rooms of Melbourne. Something must be done, and soon.

Between John Gould's observations (1852) and F. Wood Jones' (1924), the Toolache population had dwindled from "swarms" to packs of "five or six individuals." In 1923, there was a small band of 14 Toolache Wallabies on the Konetta Station. In May of that year, Professor Wood Jones desperately attempted to capture and transfer the animals to a safe sanctuary on Kangaroo Island. However, this failed because these spirited creatures literally ran themselves to death trying to escape their well-intentioned pursuers.

In 1936, Bernard C. Cotton travelled to Robe, South Australia, where he made a 16mm motion film of the Toolache Wallaby kept in a fenced paddock by Mr. J. Brown. Cotton described the animal as "probably the last living representative of its species." The remarkable film footage shows the animal running at an estimated speed of 42 miles per hour, while the voice of the narrator comments: "Note the lithe and graceful movement as portrayed by the slow motion camera."

This film footage is indeed that of the last Toolache Wallaby in existence. A handwritten note attached "in Mr Allan Rau's hand who was the South Australian Museum Taxidermist states: 'This animal died 10 July 1939 and the skin is in South Australia Museum'."

Other Australian marsupials' extinctions included: the Eastern Hare-Wallaby (*Lagorchestes leporides*) in 1890, Gilbert's Potoroo (*Potorous gilberti*) in 1900, Pig-footed Bandicoot *(Chaeropus ecaudatus)* in 1907, Western Barred Bandicoot (*Perameles mysura*) in 1910, Greater Rabbit Bandicoot or Bilby (*Macrotis lagatis grandis*) in 1930, and Eastern Barred Bandicoot (*Perameles fasciata*) in 1940.

Australia's smallest Kangaroo, the miniature (one foot tall) Parma White-Fronted Wallaby, was believed to have been exterminated in 1932. Its rediscovery in 1966 was greeted with some celebration. In the wake of this discovery, a local politician made a well-meaning, but somewhat puzzling, pledge on behalf of the Australian Government. "The Parma Wallaby," he declared, "will never be allowed to become extinct again."

THIRD WATCH   2 A.M.   MIDNIGHT

# PRAYER OF THE WINABARAKU

Toolache Wallaby or Winabaraku – 1940

1.

Now the All-Father thought
There should be sky

There should be mountains
And there should be sea

There should be beasts on the plain
And birds in the trees

There should be fish in the lakes
And creatures in the sea

So He made them
And for this we give thanks


2.

Now the All-Father thought
In this time and in this place

There should be the Winabaraku

So He made us – and we arose
Like a desert spring in flood time

In the land of salt marsh
And the stringy bark tree

And for this we give thanks

3.

Now the All-Father thought
In this time and in this place

All He did and made
Must come to an end

In the land of salt marsh
And the stringy bark tree

So like a desert spring in drought time
We descend to deep caverns far below

And for this we give thanks

# THE GREAT BUFFALO HUNT

# AMERICAN BLACK BISON – 1825
## Bison bison pennsylvanicus

Hernando Cortez – 1581
### De Solis: History of Conquest, Mexico

In the second Square of the same House were the Wild Beasts, captured by Montezuma's Hunters, in strong Cages of Timber, ranged in good Order, and under Cover: Lions, Tygers, Bears, and all others of the savage Kind which New-Spain produced; among which the greatest Rarity was the Mexican Bull; a wonderful composition of divers animals. It has crooked Shoulders, with a Bunch on its Back like a Camel; its Flanks dry, its Tail large, and its Neck covered with Hair like a Lion. It is cloven footed, its Head armed like that of a Bull, which it resembles in Fierceness, with no less strength and Agility.

Hernando Cortez's 1521 sighting of the Bison – or American Buffalo – in Montezuma's menagerie is the first by a European as recorded by the historian De Solis in 1724. It was probably captured in the northern Mexican state of Coahuila, some 500 miles north of Montezuma's palace in what is now Mexico City. In 1530, another Spaniard, Alvar Nunez Cabeza, was wrecked on the Gulf coast, west of the Mississippi delta, from whence he wandered westward into what is now Texas. He appears to be the first European to sight bison herds in their wild state.

In 1542, the conquistador Coronado was the third European to record the sighting of American Buffalo. In the region of the Texas panhandle he saw for the first time what he described as "crooked-backed oxen." It was also a notable first encounter between bison and horses. The event is described by one of Coronado's soldiers, Castenada: "The first time we encountered these beasts, all the horses took to flight on seeing them, for they were a horrible sight. They have a broad and short face, eyes two palms from each other, and projecting in such a manner sideways that they can see a pursuer. Their beard is like that of goats, and so long that it drags the ground when they lower the head. They have, on the anterior portion of the body, a frizzled hair like sheep's wool; it is very fine upon the croup, and sleek like a lion's mane. Their horns are very short and thick, and can scarcely be seen through the hair. They always change their hair in May, and at this season they really resemble lions. Their tail is very short, and terminates in a great tuft. When they run they carry it in the air like scorpions."

Samuell Argoll – 1612
## *Voyage to the New World,* Virginia Colony

And then marching into the Countrie, I found great store of Cattle as big as Kine, of which the Indians that were my guides killed a couple, which we found to be very good and wholesome meate, and are very easie to be killed, in regard they are heavy, slow, and not so wild as other beasts of the wilderness.

The English navigator Samuell Argoll wrote of this encounter with an Eastern bison that saved his party from starvation. It is the earliest recorded sighting of the Eastern Black Bison and took place in 1612 on the banks of the Potomac River, near the present-day site of America's capitol, Washington, D.C.

There were once four subspecies of Bison or American Buffalo which numbered in the hundreds of millions. The tallest and largest was the now extinct Black Bison (*Bison bison pennsylvanicus*). Found in all the American states east of the Mississippi River, it was the first to be hunted to extinction by 1825. The second species to suffer extinction was the far western Oregon Bison (*Bison bison oreganos*) around 1850 – shortly after the Lewis and Clark expedition established the Oregon Trail, and opened the region (Oregon to California) west of the Rocky Mountains for settlement. The two other races, the Great Plains Bison (*Bison bison bison*) of America and the Wood Bison (*Bison bison athabasca*) of Canada, would certainly have been entirely extinguished by 1890 had it not been for an 11th hour rescue effort by the American and Canadian governments at the instigation of the handful of influential conservationists who formed the American Bison Society.

Colonel Daniel Boone – 1770
*Frontier Journals,* **Kentucky**

Vast herds grazed over these lands. The buffaloes were more frequent than I have seen cattle in the settlements, browsing on the leaves of the cane, or cropping the herbage of those extensive plains, fearless because ignorant of the violence of man. Sometimes we saw thousands in a drove, and the numbers about the salt springs were amazing. Their ways are as beaten as our great roads, and no herb grows therein.

The wildlife artist James Audubon wrote of the Black Bison of the Eastern American states in his *Quadrupeds of North America*: "In the days of our boyhood and youth, Buffaloes roamed over the small and beautiful prairies of Indiana and Illinois, and herds of them stalked through the open woods of Kentucky and Tennessee; but they had dwindled down to a few stragglers, which resorted chiefly to the 'Barrens', towards the years 1808 and 1809, and soon after entirely disappeared.

"Their range has since that period gradually tended westward, and now you must direct your steps 'to the Indian country', and travel many hundreds of miles beyond the fair valleys of the Ohio, towards the great rocky chain of mountains that forms the backbone of North America, before you can reach the Buffalo, and see him roving in his sturdy independence upon the vast elevated plains, which extend to the base of the Rocky Mountains."

Another contemporary account of the hunting of the Eastern Black Bison by M. Ashe records the obvious reason for their demise: "The carnage of these beasts was everywhere the same. I met with a man who had killed two thousand buffaloes with his own hand, and others no doubt have done the same thing. In consequence of such proceedings not one buffalo is at this time to be found east of the Mississippi."

Colonel Richard Irving Dodge – 1871
*Plains of the Great West,* **Arkansas**

In May of 1871, I drove a light wagon from Old Fort Zara to Fort Larned, on the Arkansas. At least 25 miles of this distance was through one immense herd, composed of countless smaller herds of buffalo. The whole country appeared one great mass of buffalo, moving slowly to the northward. When I had reached a point where the hills were no longer more than a mile from the road, the buffalo on the hills, turned, stared an instant, then started at full speed directly towards me, stampeding and bringing with them the numberless herds through which they passed, and pouring down upon me all the herds, in one immense compact mass of plunging animals, mad with fright, and as irresistible as an avalanche. This situation was by no means pleasant.

In later years, Colonel Dodge reflected on the reasons for the rapid extinction of those vast migrating herds: "It was, then, the hide-hunters, who wiped out the great southern herd in four short years. The prices received for hides varied considerably, according to circumstances, but for the green or undressed article it usually ranged from 50 cents for the skins of calves to $1.25 for those of adult animals in good condition. Such prices seem ridiculously small, but when it is remembered that, when buffaloes were plentiful it was no uncommon thing for a hunter to kill from forty to sixty head a day, it will readily be seen that the chances of making very handsome profits were sufficient to tempt hunters to make extraordinary exertions.

"Moreover, even when the buffalo were nearly gone, the country was overrun with men who had absolutely nothing else to look as a means of livelihood, and so, no matter whether the profits were great or small, so long as enough buffaloes remained to make it possible to get a living by their pursuit, they were hunted down with the most determined persistency and pertinacity."

Colonel Dodge's estimate of buffalo slaughtered in southern herd for the years 1872 to 1874 was 3,698,730 (of which more than half were killed and wasted, without taking hides or meat). By 1875, less than 10,000 survived, and these were soon gone.

General Philip H. Sheridan – 1878
*Sheridan's Memoirs,* **Indian Territories**

The Buffalo Hunters have done more in the last two years to settle the vexed Indian Question than the entire regular army in the last thirty years. They have destroyed the Indian's commissary. Send them powder and lead, if you will, and let them kill, skin and sell until they have exterminated the buffalo.

General Sheridan voices the deliberate policy of the American military and government of promoting the extermination of the buffalo herds of the west as a means of starving the native Indian tribes into submission.

Congressman McCormick wrote in *The New Mexican* newspaper in Santa Fe that a United States federal surveying commission kept careful records of the slaughter and reported that there were two thousand hunters on the plains killing these animals for their hides. One party of sixteen hunters was reported having killed twenty-eight thousand buffaloes in the summer of 1872 in supposedly Indian Territories.

Sheridan absolutely encouraged the poaching of buffalo and the invasion of the Indian Territories. He suggested Congress mint a medal of honour for the hunters with a dead buffalo on one side and a depressed looking Indian on the other. He was widely attributed with the saying, "The only good Indian is a dead Indian."

The other ex-Civil War soldier assigned to oversee Indian Affairs policy was General William Tecumseh Sherman. In a letter to President Grant, Sherman wrote: "We are not going to let a few thieving Indians check or stop progress. We must act with vindictive earnest against the Sioux, even to their extermination, men, women and children." Sherman also saw killing off the buffalo as the means of starving Indians into submission.

FIRST WATCH / 3 A.M. \ VEIL

# CITIES OF GOLD

American Black Bison – 1825

Coronado searching for the Seven Cities of Gold
Marched through Arizona and New Mexico

Seeking the legendary Cibolo
With its streets and roofs of gold
Its walls studded with gems

Discovered instead Zuni and Pueblo
Villages of rough-cut stone and adobe

Embittered and raging with greed
Coronado waded across the Rio Grande

Stubbed his steel toe on the Grand Canyon
Butchered and burned his way across Texas

Dodging Apache and Comanche arrows
The Spaniard stamped on into Kansas
In his relentless quest for Gran Quivera

That other chimeric promised land
With its mother lode of fabled gold

Coronado looking for shining spires
Found instead a vast plain crowded with beasts
"Horned, huge and monstrously ugly"

A dark satanic host – the very scent
Of which terrorized his horses

Denied the spectacular glory
Of Aztec gold, of Inca silver

Bloodied Coronado limped home in shame
With a wagon train heaped with the skins
Of those "crook-backed oxen"

Those same buffalo robes that were to become
The true currency of the wilderness

Triggering a stampede into the long darkness
That would eclipse all life on that great wide plain

And from the bones of those millions and millions
Sown like dragons teeth into the parched earth
There arose seven cities; and seven cities more

Richer than the greediest dreams
Of Coronado's conquistadors

These Cities of Gold, these New Eldorados
Shimmer in the sun

And yet, when darkness falls
On the empty plains beyond city lights

For some, there is this lingering memory
Of the distant thunder of those endless herds

And the last of the Ghost Dancers
Dressed in buffalo robes, chanting:

>    *Nothing lives forever*
>    *Nothing lives forever*
>
>    *Except the earth and the sky*
>    *Nothing lives forever*

# THE BLUE METEOR

# PASSENGER PIGEON OR MIGRATING DOVE – 1914
## *Ectopistes migratorius*

Jacques Cartier – 1534
### *Voyages de Jacques Cartier,* New France

On 1 July 1534, Jacques Cartier in his ship's log – as reported in his *Voyages de Jacques Cartier* – recorded the first written European sighting of a vast flock of Passenger Pigeons just off the coast of what is now Prince Edward Island. Cartier's description is here whimsically translated in the form of a haiku:

> "The sky darkens
> with an infinite multitude
> of wild blue pigeons."

In 1605, another French explorer, Samuel de Champlain, in his ship's log – as reported in his *Voyages de Samuel de Champlain* – made the second French sighting of a vast flock of Passenger Pigeons just off the coast of Maine. Champlain's log entry is similarly succinct, and like Cartier's is here ironically translated as a haiku:

> "There are countless doves
> whereof we knock down and take
> a goodly number."

There followed a number of early descriptions of these birds in "New France" written by the missionaries. Among them, Gabriel Sagard-Théodat, in his *Le Grand Voyage du pays des Hurons* of 1632: "There are here an endless multitude of doves, which the Huron call 'Orittey' that feed in part on acorns which they easily swallow whole. In the beginning they were so stupid that they allowed themselves to be knocked down by blows of stones and poles from beneath the trees, but at present they are a little more wary."

And again from "New France," in 1663, in the records known as the *Jesuit Relations and Allied Documents*, we find: "Among the birds of every variety to be found here, it is to be noted that Pigeons abound in such numbers that this year one man killed a hundred and thirty-two at a single shot. They passed continually in flocks so dense, and so near the ground, that sometimes they were struck down with oars."

SECOND WATCH 4 A.M. VEIL

William Strachey – 1612
**Letters, Virginia Colony**

A kind of wood-pidgeon we see here in the winter time, and of such numbers, as I should drawe the creditt of my relation concerning all the other in question, yf I should expresse what extended flocks, and how manie thousands in one flock, I have seen in one daie, wondering (I must confesse) at their flight, when, like so many thickned clowdes, they (having fed to the northward in the day tyme) retourne againe more sowardly towards night to their roust; but there be manie hundred witnesses, who maie convince this my report, yf herein yt testifieth an untruth.

In 1614, two years after William Strachey, we have another record of Passenger Pigeons in the letters of the Governor of the Virginia Colony, Sir Thomas Dale: "There are wilde Pidgeons in Winter beyond number or imagination, my selfe have scene three or four houres together flockes in the Aire, so thicke that even they have shadowed the Skie from us."

A similar observation was made in 1625 in Nicolas-Jean de Wassenaer's *First Settlement of New Netherlands* (in what is now Manhattan, New York City): "The Birds most common are wild Pigeons; these are so numerous that they shut out the sunshine."

William Wood – 1634
*Wood's New England Prospect*

These Birds come into the Countrey, in the beginning of our Spring, at which time (if I may be counted worthy, to be believed in a thing that is not so strange as true) I have seen them fly as if the Ayerie regiment had been Pigeons; seeing neyther beginning nor ending, in length, or breadth of these Millions of Millions. The shouting of people, the ratling of Gunnes, and the pelting of small shotte could not drive them out of their course, but so they continued for foure or five houres together. Many of them build amongst the Pine-trees, thirty miles to the North-east of our plantations; joyning nest to nest, and tree to tree by their nests, so the Sunne never sees the ground in that place, from whence the Indians fetch whole loades of them.

In 1648, the Governor of New England, John Winthrop, recorded in his *The History of New England*: "This month, when our first harvest was near had in, the pigeons came again all over the country, but did no harm, (harvest being just in,) but proved a great blessing, it being incredible what multitudes of them were killed daily. It was ordinary for one man to kill eight or ten dozen in half a day, yea five or six dozen at one shoot, and some seven or eight. Thus the Lord showed us, that he could make the same creature, which formerly had been a great chastisement, now become a great blessing."

Nearly a century after Strachey's observations, the numbers of Passenger Pigeons do not seem to have diminished in the New England Colonies, as suggested in Cotton Mather's account in his *The Christian Philosopher*: "I will add a Curiousity relating to the Pidgeons, which annually visit my own Country in their Seasons, in such incredible numbers, that they have commonly been sold for Two-pence a dozen; Yea, one Man has at one time surprised no less than two hundred dozen in his Barn, into which they have come for Food, and by shutting the door, he has had them all."

SECOND WATCH | 4 A.M. | VEIL

John James Audubon – 1813
*Ornithological Biography*, **Kentucky**

I cannot describe to you the extreme beauty of their aerial evolutions, at once, like a torrent, and with noise like thunder, they rushed into a compact mass, pressing each other towards the centre. In these almost solid masses, they darted forward in undulating and angular lines, descended and swept close over the earth with inconceivable velocity, mounted perpendicularly so as to resemble a vast column, and, when high, were seen wheeling and twisting with their continued lines, which then resembled the coils of a gigantic serpent.

In his Louisville, Kentucky *Journals*, Audubon wrote: "In autumn of 1813, I left my house at Henderson, on the banks of the Ohio, on my way to Louisville. The air was literally filled with Pigeons; the light of the sun was obscured as by an eclipse; and the continued buzz of wings had a tendency to lull my senses to repose.... Before sunset I reached Louisville, distant from Henderson fifty-five miles, the Pigeons were still passing in undiminished numbers, and continued to do so for three days in succession." Audubon estimated the size of this flock over Louisville as "one billion, one hundred and fifteen million, one hundred and thirty-six thousand pigeons."

John James Audubon – 1814
*Ornithological Biography,* **Kentucky**

Let us now, kind Reader, inspect their place of nightly rendezvous. I arrived there nearly two hours before sunset. Few Pigeons were then to be seen, but a great number of persons, with horses and wagons, guns and ammunition, had already established encampments on the borders. Many trees two feet in diameter, I observed broken off at no great distance from the ground; and the branches of many of the largest and tallest had given way, as if the forest had been swept by a tornado. As the period of their arrival approached, their foes anxiously prepared to receive them. Some were furnished with iron-pots containing sulphur, others were with torches of pine-knots, many with poles, and the rest with guns. Suddenly there burst forth a general cry of: "Here they come!" The noise they made, though yet distant, reminded me of a hard gale at sea, passing through the rigging of a close-reefed vessel. As the birds arrived and passed over me, I felt a current of air that surprised me. Thousands were soon knocked down by the pole-men. The birds continued to pour in. The fires were lighted, and a magnificent, as well as wonderful and almost terrifying sight presented itself. The Pigeons, arriving by thousands, alighted everywhere, one above another, until solid masses as large as hogsheads were formed on the branches all round. Here and there the perches gave way under the weight with a crash, and falling to the ground, destroying hundreds of birds beneath, forcing down the dense groups with which every stick was loaded. It was a scene of uproar and confusion. I found it quite useless to speak, or shout to those who were nearest to me. Even the reports of the guns were seldom heard, and I was made aware of the firing only by seeing the shooters reloading.

Audubon describes the aftermath of slaughter in this 1814 nesting site: "No one dared venture within the line of devastation. The Pigeons were constantly coming, and it was past midnight before I perceived a decrease in the number of those that arrived. The uproar continued the whole night. Towards the approach of day, the noise in some measure subsided, long before objects were distinguishable, pigeons began to move off, and at sunrise all that were able to fly had disappeared."

SECOND WATCH / 4 A.M. / VEIL

James Fenimore Cooper – 1823
*The Pioneers,* New York

If the heavens were alive with pigeons, the whole village seemed equally in motion, with men, women, and children. Every species of fire-arms from the French ducking-gun with a barrel near six feet in length, to the common horseman's pistol, was in the hands of the men and boys; while bows and arrows, and others in rude imitation of cross-bows, were carried by many. So prodigious was the number of the birds, that the scattering fire of the guns, with the hurling of missiles, and the cries of the boys, had no other effect than to break off small flocks from the immense masses that continued to dart along the valley, as if the whole of the feathered tribe were pouring through that one pass. None pretended to collect the game, which lay scattered over the fields in such profusion as to cover the very ground with the fluttering victims.

The Massachusettes State Ornithologist Edward Forbush recorded this account of Chief Pokagon, the last Pottawottomi chief, describing an approaching flock of Passenger Pigeons while camping on the Manistee River in Michigan: "One morning I was startled by hearing a gurgling, rumbling sound, as though an army of horses laden with sleigh bells was advancing through the deep forests toward me. As I listened intently, I concluded that instead of the tramping of horses it was distant thunder; and yet the morning was clear, calm and beautiful. Nearer and nearer came the strange commingling of sleigh bells mixed with an approaching storm. While I gazed in wonder and astonishment I beheld moving before me in an unbroken front millions of pigeons."

William Dunlop – 1832
*A Backwoodsman,* Toronto

For three or four days the town resounded with one continuous roll of firing, as if a skirmish were going on in the streets. Every gun, pistol, musket, blunderbuss, and firearm of whatever description, was put in requisition. The constable and police were on the alert, and offenders without number were pulled up. Among them were honourable members of the executive and legislative counsel, crown lawyers, respectable staid citizens, and last of all, the sheriff of the county; till at last it was found that pigeons, flying within easy shot, were a temptation too strong for human virtue to withstand; and so the contest was given up and a sporting jubilee proclaimed to all and sundry.

> Some professional hunters used huge net traps baited with decoy birds, known as "stool pigeons." These captured birds had their eyes sewn shut and their legs pinned to a post or "stool." Acorns were then strewn about the netted area, and when a flock passed over, the stool was pulled out from under the blind bird, which would flutter its wings to land. The fluttering wings made it appear that the bird was landing and safely feeding. Birds from the passing flock would be lured into landing, and thousands of birds could be caught at once in the huge spring-loaded butterfly nets and slaughtered.

John Frost – 1848
*Game Birds of America,* New York

None of the names bestowed upon this species are sufficiently descriptive of it. '*Passenger*', an English expression, and '*migratoria*', the Latin name, fall equally short, inasmuch as every known pigeon is to a greater or less extent migratory. The '*swarm*' pigeon, the '*flood*' pigeon, or even the '*deluge*' pigeon would be a more appropriate appellation; for the weight of their numbers breaks down the forest with scarcely less havoc than if the stream of the Mississippi were poured upon it.

By 1860, pigeon hunting became a full time occupation for several thousand men. With the advent of the telegraph and the railroad, hunters were able to follow and slaughter the migrating birds wherever they landed. By 1896, virtually the entire surviving population of Passenger Pigeons came together in one last great nesting outside Bowling Green, Ohio near Mammoth Caves. The entire nesting was slaughtered and loaded in boxcars, but due to a derailment, the hunters' efforts were wasted: rotting carcasses of all 200,000 birds had to be dumped in a deep ravine a few miles from the railway loading yard.

On 24 March 1900 in Pike County, Ohio, the last wild Passenger Pigeon was shot by a young boy. On 1 September 1914 in the Cincinnati Zoo, "Martha," a passenger pigeon born in captivity, died aged 29 years. She was the last of her species. Four years later – on 21 February 1918 – in the same pagoda aviary in the Cincinnati Zoo, the last Carolina Parakeet (*Conuropsis carolinensis*), named Incas, died at age 32.

# TROJANS

## Passenger Pigeon or Migratory Dove – 1914

1.

There is no epic poem for the Passenger Pigeon
No Iliad or Aeneid. No requiem. No lament

Yet, billions in flight once eclipsed the sun
Brought darkness and chaos at midday
To New York, Boston and Philadelphia
To Montreal, Chicago and New Orleans

The longest and swiftest of the world's pigeons
It measured a foot and a half – beak to tail
Beautifully stream-lined and steel blue
Mile-a-minute flash across the open sky

The whole of forested America was its empire
From the Arctic tree line to the Caribbean Sea

The greatest natural wonder of the New World
Its annual migrations – the greatest congregations
Of birds ever gathered on the planet

The extinction of this feathered tribe
Is as much our brutal legacy
As the extinction of the Trojans
Was the savage heritage of the Greeks

And after their annihilation, came the destruction
Of the nation's beech forests by axe and fire
An act akin to the levelling of the walls of Troy

2.

Had there been a valiant Hector among their number?
Certainly there was an Astyanax among the millions
Upon millions that were hurled to their death

But there was no Aeneas to carry his father
And lead his child out of the flames

There was to be no hope of the survival
Of a royal bloodline in some distant future age

Only a pathetic huddled gathering
Like those last few enslaved Trojan Women

One last captive flock held in a cage
And displayed for the conquerors' amusement
In the Cincinnati Zoo

And yes, among them was a Hecuba
The last great queen of her race

There, in a pen open to wind and rain
Ill-fed and neglected by their keepers
The captives fell away one by one
Until only the queen remained

Without the least awareness of irony
Or intent at a final insult
Her keepers gave her the name "Martha"

After Martha Washington – mother of the nation
That exterminated her species

Nor did her humiliation end with her death
Her carcass encased in a block of ice
Was transported to the capital
Where she was eviscerated and embalmed

Denied the dignity and respect of a proper burial
Her carcass is displayed in the Smithsonian
Like a severed head on a spike

In her passing came the end
Of this great wonder of our world
As significant to us as the obliteration
Of Troy was to the Greeks

Should the memory of "Martha" haunt us
As the shade of Hecuba haunted the Greeks?

Those conquerors who – for centuries thereafter –
Would hear, in the howling desolate wind
Sweeping over the plains of the Hellespont,
The tortured wailing of that last great queen

# THE GODLESS GAME

## HEATH HEN – 1933 – *Tympanuchus cupido cupido*

Alexander Wilson – 1811
### *American Ornithology,* Wilmington, North Carolina

A sharp focus is brought to bear on the state of mind of the people of those days* when conservation was discussed. It is recorded that when the chairman read the name of the bill "*An Act for the Preservation Of the Heath-Hen and Other Game*", the northern members were astonished and could not see the propriety of preserving "*Indians or any other heathen*".

* State Legislature, New York – 1791

> Heath Hens inhabited nearly the whole of the open prairie from Maine to Pennsylvania. They bred and fed in groupings of several thousand strong and the plain was alive in springtime with the characteristic uproar of hundreds of males "booming" their mating dance. This made them easy targets for market hunters, and Wilson notes that the price of a brace of grouse over 20 years after 1800 went up from $1 to $5. Despite its obvious immanent obliteration, no measures were taken to preserve it, and it became extinct in New York State, Pennsylvania, and mainland New England by 1844. A sternum bone in New York's American Museum of Natural History is the only evidence of the bird's having once lived in New York State.

Thomas Nuttal – 1840

*An Ornithologist's Journal,* Boston, Massachusetts

Not long ago, the Heath Hen had been so common on the ancient brushy site of Boston, that servants stipulated with their employers not to have Heath Hen brought to the table oftener than a few times a week. In western Massachusetts the last bird was shot in 1830, and is all but extinct on the mainland. It is now only protected on the island of Martha's Vineyard.

In 1890, there were an estimated 200 surviving Heath Hens – all on the island of Martha's Vineyard. However, by 1908, these were down to 50 when a 1600 acre reserve was set aside for them, and their numbers rose dramatically by 1915 to 2000. It appeared as if the species would survive, but in 1916 the population dropped to 150; and by 1925 there were only 20 remaining. By 1930, there was only a single male until, at the age of 8, it vanished forever on the evening of 11 March 1933.

New Zealand's only indigenous game bird was the once numerous New Zealand Quail or Koreke (*Coturnix novaezelandiae*). This bird suffered depletion of numbers through over-hunting for food and sport, but the final extirpation was only achieved through the efforts of Sir Walter Buller, New Zealand's foremost ornithologist. Keen to acquire specimens of the near-extinct species, in 1868 near Blueskin Bay, Buller discovered a covey of twenty birds. In the name of science, Buller shot every one of them: the last twenty Koreke in existence.

The most remarkable and unique species of game bird to become extinct in the last couple of centuries has to be the Bengali Pink-Headed Duck (*Rhodensessa caryophyllacea*). In Bengali it was called the *Saknal*; in Hindustani *Golabi-sir*; in Tirhoot *Umar*; and in Nepalese *Dumrar*. Once thought to be a true freshwater duck (genus *Anas*), it later was assigned a genus unto itself, *Rhodenessa*. It was not only unique in having a pink head and neck, but was also the only duck to lay perfectly spherical eggs. Extinguished in the wild by 1935, the last Pink-Headed Duck died in captivity in Fitzwarren Park, England in 1942.

Another unique species of waterfowl and game bird was a sea-duck that once inhabited the Atlantic coast of Canada and America. This was the strikingly parti-coloured Labrador Duck (*Camptorhynchus labradorius*), which was also called the Pied Duck and Skunk Duck because of its distinctive black and white markings. Like the Pink-Headed Duck, it was the only bird of its genus, *Camptorhynchus*. The Labrador Duck was last seen and shot on Long Island in 1875.

Arthur Beetle Hough – 1933
*Vineyard Gazette,* **Martha's Vineyard, Massachusetts**

The Heath Hen failed to adapt to changing conditions and fell victim to the laws of natural selection. This is a curious thing, for until the white men took over the land, the Heath Hen had achieved an admirable adaptation, embodying such fine distinctions of nature that scientists appreciate their nicety and would like to understand them better. Even if you knew where a Heath Hen was, against a background of twigs and brush, you could not see it unless it moved. Failed to adapt! Why, no creature was ever more at home, more nicely adjusted to place and time than the Heath Hen on the Vineyard plains! The whole trouble lay in the fact that the Heath Hen was a bird man could kill, and so it had to die. The extinction of the Heath Hen has taken away part of the magic of Martha's Vineyard. This is the added loss of the island. There is a void in the April dawn, there is an expectancy unanswered, there is a tryst not kept.

This moving obituary for the Heath Hen was published in the *Vineyard Gazette* on April 21, 1933 by the newspaper's owner, Arthur Beetle Hough.

# THE STREAM OF LIFE*

## Heath Hen – 1933

**Arthur Beetle Hough**
*Vineyard Gazette*


Now we know there are degrees
Even in death.

All around us nature is full of casualties,
But they do not interrupt the stream of life.

Yet, to the Heath Hen something
More than death has happened,
Or, rather, a different kind of death.

There is no survivor, there is no future,
There is no life to be created in this form again.

We are looking upon the uttermost finality
Which can be written,

Glimpsing the darkness which will not know
Another ray of light.

We are in touch
With the reality of extinction.


* As an elegy to the Heath Hen, I found I could do no better
than construct a "found poem" from final lines of Arthur Beetle
Hough's 1933 obituary of the Heath Hen. This is the only found
poem chosen to serve as an elegy in this collection, and is as
emotionally moving as it is profoundly thoughtful about "the
reality of extinction."

# BIBLIOGRAPHY

ALLEN, G.M. 1947 Extinct and Vanishing Mammals of the Western Hemisphere. Spec. Publ. Am. Comm. Internat. Wildlife Protection, 11. New York.

AMADON, D. 1950 The Hawaiian honeycreepers (Drepaniidae). Bull. Amer. Mus. Nat. Hist. 95, 157-257.

ANONYMOUS [probably Tafforet] 1726 Relation de l'Île de Rodrigue. [Ms. In Ministère de la Marine, Paris]. Quoted in Hacisuka, op. cit. and in Strickland & Melville, and Vinson, op. cit. infra.

ARNOLD, E. N. 1979 Indian Ocean giant tortoises: their systematica and island adaptations. Phil. Trans. Roy. Soc. Lond. B 286 127-146.

ARNOLD, E. N. 1980 Recently extinct reptile populations from Mauritius and Réunion, Indian Ocean. Jour. Zool., London 191 33-47.

AUDUBON, J. J. L. & BACHMAN, J. 1854 Quadrupeds of North America, 3 vol. New York.

BALES, S. L. & TANNER, N. 2007 Ghost Birds: Jim Tanner and the Quest for the Ivory-billed Woodpecker, 1935-1941. Knoxville: University of Tennessee.

BEECHEY, F. W. & VIGORS, N. A. 1839 The zoology of Captain Beechey's vogage to the Pacific…in the Blossom…1825 1828. London.

BERGER, A. J. 1972 Hawaiian Birdlife. Honolulu: University Press of Hawaii.

BODDAERT, P. 1785 Elenchus Animalium, Rotterdam.

BOWES, A. J. 1787-89 A journal of voyage from Portsmouth to New South Wales and China in the Lady Penrhyn.

BROWN, R. 1973 Has the Thylacine really vanished? Animals, 15.

BRYDEN, H.A. (Ed.) 1899 Great and Small Game of Africa. London.

CHAMBERS, P. 2004 A Sheltered Life: the Unexpected Life of the Giant Tortoise. London: John Murray.

DELACOUR, J. 1954 The Waterfowl of the World. 4 vol. London: Country Life.

DUBOIS, LE SIEUR. 1669 Journal. Proc. Zool. Soc. Lond. 1884.

DU TERTRE, J. B. 1667-71 Histoire générale des Antilles habitées par les Francois, 4 vol. (in 3). Paris.

FINN, F. 1915 Wild Animals of Yesterday and To-Day. London.

FISHER, J., SIMON, N. & VINCENT, J. (Eds) 1969 The Red Book. [IUCN data]. London. Collins.

FORSHAW, J. M. 1973 Parrots of the World. Melborne: Landsdowne. New York: Doubleday.

FORSTER, J. R. 1778 Observations made during a voyage round the world… London. [German edition, slightly expanded: 1779 Berlin.]

FULLER, E. 2001 Extinct Birds. Ithaca, New York: Cornell University Press.

GÉRARD, J. 1861 Lion Hunting and Sporting Life in Algeria. (Gustave Doré, illus.) London.

GIBSON, G. 2009 The Bedside Book of Beasts. Toronto: Doubleday.

GMELIN, S.G. 1774 Reise durch Russland, St. Petersburgh.

GOODWIN, D. 1970 Pigeons and Doves of the World. London: British Museum (Natural History).

GOULD, J. 1840-48 The Birds of Australia, 7 vol. [Supplements 1-5, 1851-69]. London. 1845-63 The Mammals of Australia, 3 vol. London.

GRADY, W. 2007 Bringing Back the Dodo. Toronto: McClelland and Stewart.

GRANT, C. 1801 History of Mauritius. [Deals with all Mascarene Islands]. London.

GREENWAY, J. C. Jr. 1967 Extinct and Vanishing Birds of the World, second, revised edition. New York: Dover.

GRIEVE, S. 1885 The great auk, or a garefowl…its history, archaeology, and remains. London.

GUILDER, E. R. 1961 The former Distribution and Decline of the Thylacine. Aust. Hour. Sci. 23 (7). 1966 In pursuit of the Thylacine. Oryx, August 1966.

GUNTHER, A. 1877 The Gigantic Land-Tortoises (Living and Extinct) London: Taylor & Francis.

GUNTHER, A. & HUME, J. 2008 Lost Land of the Dodo London: A.C. Black.

HACHISUKA, M. 1953 The Dodo and Kindred Birds. London: Witherby.

HALL, R.L. & SHARP, H 1978 Wolf and Man, evolution in parallel. New York: Academic Press.

HALLIDAY, T. 1978 Vanishing Birds: Their Natural History and Conservation. London: Sidgwick & Jackson. New York: Holt, Rinehart & Winston.

HARMANSEN, HEEMSKERCK, MATALEIF, SCHOUTEN, SPILBERBEN, VAN DEN ROECKE, VAN DER HAGEN & NECKE. 1702-06 Receuil des Voiages qui ont servi à l'établissement…de la Compagnie des Indes Orientales… [French trans of Dutch Journals], 5 vol. Amsterdam.

HARPER, F. 1945 Extinct and Vanishing Mammals of the Old World. Spec. Publ. Am. Comm. Internat. Wildlife Protection, 12. New York.

HERBERT, T. 1638 Some Yeares' Travaile into divers parts of Asia and Afrique… Revised and enlarged by the Author. London.

HINDWOOD, K. A. 1932 An historic diary. Emu, 32, 17-29.

HINDWOOD, K. A. 1938 The Extinct Birds of Lord Howe Island. Austr. Mag. 6, 319-324.

HONEGGER, R. E. 1981 List of Amphibians and Reptiles Either Known or Thought to Have Become Extinct since 1600. Biol. Conserv. 19, 141-158.

HOOSE, P. 2004 Race to Save the Lord God Bird. New York: Farrar, Strauss.

IUCN (International Union for Conservation of Nature and Natural Resources) Derniers Refuges. (Atlas). Brussels: Elsevier.

IUCN Red Data Books (Fish, Reptiles & Amphibians, Birds Plants and Mammals). Continuously updated SCMU (Species Conservation Monitoring Unit), 219c Huntingdon Rd., Cambridge, UK.

JOHNSGAARD, P. A. 1973 Grouse and Quails of North America. Lincoln: University of Nebraska Press.

JONES, F. W. 1924 The Mammals of South Australia. Adelaide.

LEGUAT, F. 1708 Voyages et Aventures de Francois Leguat, & de ses Compagnons, en deux isles désertes de Indes Orientales... 2 vol. London. [English, 1 vol., trans: A New Voyage to the East Indies by Francis Leguat and his companions, 1708. London].

LOPEZ, B. H. 1978 Of Wolves and Men. London: Dent. 1979. New York: Scribner.

LYDEKKER, R. 1912 The Horse and its Relatives, London: George Allen and Unwin.

MACFARLAND, C. G.,VILLA, J.& TORO, B. 1974 The Galapagos giant tortoises (Geochelone elephantopus). Part 1: Status of the surviving populations. Biol. Conserv. 6 118–133.

MECH, D. 1970 The Wolf. New York: Doubleday.

NORTH-COOMBES, A. 1971 The Island of Rodigues. Port Louis, Mauritius: privately printed.

OLIVER, W.R.B. 1949 Moas of New Zealand. Dominion Museum Bulletin, 15. Wellington.

OLIVER, W.R.B. 1955 New Zealand Birds. Wellington: Reed.

OWEN, C. 2001 The Wrecks of Eden. Toronto: Wolsak and Wynn.

PADDIE, R. 2000 The Last Tasmanian Tiger. Cambridge.

POCOCK, R.I. 1913 The affinities of the Antarctic Wolf. Proc. Zool. Soc. London, 382 393.

POLIAKOV, I.S. 1881 Isvestia Russki Geographischeski. St. Peterburg 17: 1-20.

RADDE, G. 1893 On the present range of the European Bison in the Caucasus. Proc. Zool. Soc. London.

RIDE, W.D.I. 1970 Guide to the Native Mammals of Australia. London: Oxford University Press.

RIPLEY, S.D. 1952 Vanishing and extinct bird species of India. Journ. Bombay Nat. Hist. Soc. 50 (4) 902-906.

RIPLEY, S.D. 1977 Rails of the World. Toronto: Feheley.

ROTHCHILD, L.W.R. 1907 Extinct birds. London: Hutchinson and Co.

SCARLETT, R.J. 1974 Moa and Man in New Zealand. Notornis, 21 (1).

SCHORGER, A.W. 1955 The Passenger Pigeon. Madison: University of Wisconsin.

SHELDON, C. 1912 Wilderness of the North Pacific Coast Islands, London.

SHOEMAKER, H.W. 1915 A Pennsylvania bison hunt. Middleburg, Pa.

SILVERBURG, W.S. 1969 The Auk, the Dodo and the Oryx: vanished and vanishing creatures. Tadworth, Surrey: World's Work.

SMITH, C.H. 1841 The Natural History of Horses, Edinburgh.

STEJNEGER, L. 1936 Georg Wilhelm Steller, the pioneer of Alaskan Natural History. Cambridge, Mass. Harvard University Press.

STREET, P. 1961 Vanishing animals: preserving nature's rarities. London: Faber.

STRESEMAN, E. 1950 Birds collected during Capt. James Cook's last expedition (1776-1780) Auk, 67, 66-88.

STRICKLAND, H.E. & MELVILLE, A.G. 1848 The Dodo and its kindred... London.

SWENK, M.H. 1916 The Eskimo Curlew and its disappearance. Ann. Rep. Smithsonian Inst. For 1915, 325-340.

TANNER, J. T. 1942 The ivory-billed woodpecker. Reprint. New York: Dover.

TEMPLE, S.A. 1974 Last Chance to Save Round Island. Wildlife, Summer 1974.

THOMPSON, A.L. 1964 A New Dictionary of Birds. London: Nelson.

VAN DENBURGH, J. 1914 The gigantic land tortoises of the Galapagos archipelago. Proc. Calif. Acad. Sci. 2, 203-374.

VINSON, J. & VINSON, J.M. 1969 The Saurian Fauna of the Mascarene Islands. Maur. Inst. Bull. 6 (4), 2103-320.

WALTERS, M. 1980 The Complete Birds of the World. London: David & Charles.

WARNER, R.E. 1968 The Role of Introduced Diseases in the Extinction of the Endemic Hawaiian Avifauna. Condor, 70.

WATERHOUSE, G.R. & DARWIN, C. 1839 Zoology of the voyage of the Beagle. (Mammalia). London.

ZISWILLER, U. 1967 Extinct and Vanishing Animals, revised English edition, F. & P. Bunnell, London: Longmans Green.

# INDEX

## Principal Animals and Reportage Authors

# ACKNOWLEDGEMENTS

Many thanks to Róisín Magill for her advice and assistance in the creation of this book. Thanks also to Peter Sanger of the *Antigonish Review*, Boris Castel of *Queen's Quarterly*, Karen Mulhallen of *Descant*, and Charise Foster of *CV2* – all of whom published excerpts from *Nevermore* in their magazines. And to the late Robert Wagner, who broadcast a sequence of these poems on *CBC Radio*; as well as to the *Canada Council for the Arts*, the *Ontario Arts Council*, and the *Writer's Trust George Woodcock Fund* for their generous financial assistance.

I also wish to acknowledge my editor Allan Briesmaster for his wise counsel and patience; my designer Julie McNeill for an inspired and creative transformation of the manuscript into this beautiful book; and to the editors and staff of Quattro Books: Beatriz Hausner, John Calabro, Luciano Iacobelli, Sonia Di Placido, Lisa Young and Maddy Curry, for their enthusiastic commitment to this publication.

# ILLUSTRATION CREDITS

Maurice Wilson – pages 52, 82, 92, 106, 138, 144, 152, 158

Mick Loates – pages 5, 58, 82, 100, 178

Tim Bramfitt – pages 20, 26, 32, 64, 70, 132, 166

Peter Hayman – pages 120, 126

Augsburg Artist – page 40

Richard Lydeckker – page 46

John James Audubon – page 112

# ABOUT THE AUTHOR

David Day was born and raised in Victoria, British Columbia. His first book *The Cowichan* (based on his timber camp journals) was published in 1975. In 1978, Day published *A Tolkien Bestiary*, the first of his six internationally best-selling books on the works of J.R.R. Tolkien. Day has travelled extensively, and lived in England, Greece and Spain. He currently lives in Toronto.

David Day's landmark book on animal extinction, the *Doomsday Book of Animals* – with an introduction by the Duke of Edinburgh – was selected in 1981 as a "Book of the Year" by *Time Magazine, The Christian Science Monitor, The Los Angeles Times, The Observer*, and *New Scientist*. This was followed by the *Whale War* (1987), *Eco-Wars* (1988), *Encyclopedia of Vanished Species* (1989), and *Noah's Choice* (1990). Day has also been an environmental columnist for Britain's *Daily Mail, Evening Standard, Mail on Sunday, Sunday Times*, and *Punch Magazine*. His *Punch* columns became the books *True Tales of Environmental Madness* in 1990 and *The Complete Rhinoceros* in 1994.

In 1996 he wrote the *Lost Animals* British Channel Four and Japanese NHK TV series of one hundred five-minute documentaries on extinct species. It was narrated by the Oscar-winning actress Greta Scacchi, and later was translated into 20 languages. His *Whale War* was the basis of a British ITV documentary.

David Day has also written six illustrated books of animal stories and three illustrated books of animal poems for children. His *Emperor's Panda* was runner-up for both the Governor General's Award and the National Library Award. His CBC and National Magazine award-winning poems have been praised by both the Canadian poet Al Purdy and the British poet laureate Ted Hughes.